Teaching Your
SECONDARY ELLs
THE ACADEMIC
LANGUAGE *of* TESTS

FOCUSING ON ENGLISH LANGUAGE ARTS

Solution Tree | Press

a division of

Solution Tree

r4 Educated Solutions

Published by Solution Tree Press

555 North Morton Street
Bloomington, IN 47404
800.733.6786 (toll free) / 812.336.7700
FAX: 812.336.7790

email: info@solution-tree.com
solution-tree.com

Printed in the United States of America

Library of Congress Control Number:

13 12 11 10 09   1 2 3 4 5

Library of Congress Cataloging-in-Publication Data

Teaching your secondary English language learners the academic language
of tests : focusing on English language arts / r4 Educated Solutions.
    p. cm.
  Includes bibliographical references.
  ISBN 978-1-934009-70-3 -- ISBN 978-1-935249-03-0 (lib. ed.) 1.
English language--Study and teaching (Secondary)--Foreign speakers. 2.
English language--Study and teaching (Secondary)--Spanish speakers. 3.
Vocabulary--Study and teaching (Secondary) 4. Test-taking skills--Study
and teaching (Secondary) I. R4 Educated Solutions.
  PE1128.A2T446 2009
  428.2'4--dc22
                                    2009005222

President: Douglas Rife
Publisher: Robert D. Clouse
Director of Production: Gretchen Knapp
Managing Editor of Production: Caroline Wise
Copy Editor: Nancy Sixsmith
Text Designer: Amy Shock
Cover Designer: Pamela Rude

Acknowledgments

r4 Educated Solutions would like to acknowledge the dedication of the many Region 4 content-area specialists and external reviewers who devoted time to the development of this book. Their expertise and commitment to children produced this resource to assist educators with quality, effective classroom instruction for English language learners.

Visit **go.solution-tree.com/ELL** to download all the reproducibles in this book.

Table of Contents

Italicized entries in the Table of Contents indicate reproducible forms.

Chapter 2

Chapter 3

Teaching the Language of the Open-Ended Response 89

Chapter 4

Teaching the ELA Academic Vocabulary 115

About r4 Educated Solutions

r4 Educated Solutions is a first-choice provider for the needs of educators, schools, and districts, from cutting-edge instructional materials to assessment data visualization to efficient food service training to inventive transportation solutions. r4 Educated Solutions products and services are developed, field-tested, and implemented by the Region 4 Education Service Center (Region 4).

Region 4, located in Houston, Texas, is one of twenty service centers established by the Texas Legislature in 1967. The service centers assist school districts in improving student performance, enable school districts to operate more efficiently and economically, and implement state initiatives. Encompassing seven counties in the upper Texas Gulf Coast area, Region 4 serves fifty-four independent school districts and forty-nine state-approved charter schools. As the largest service center in Texas, Region 4 serves an educational community of over 1,000,000 students (almost one-fourth of the state's total student population), more than 83,000 professional educators, and approximately 1,300 campuses.

The core purpose of Region 4 is revolutionizing education to inspire and advance future generations. Instructional materials such as this publication are written and reviewed by content-area specialists who have an array of experience in providing quality, effective classroom instruction that provides the most impact on student achievement.

Introduction

If only they understood the question, they could answer it. They know the content; they just don't know enough English.

Teaching Your Secondary English Language Learners the Academic Language of Tests was written in response to remarks such as this one. The purpose of this manual is twofold: to provide evidence-based, teacher-friendly lesson plans that will help English language learners deal with unfamiliar language features on standardized test questions, and to support English language arts teachers in providing instruction for content-specific language skills. This manual is geared toward secondary students in grades 6–12.

Each lesson plan provides background information for the teacher, implications for high-stakes testing, a list of materials, academic vocabulary, activities, and in many cases, graphic organizers. Some of the lesson plans support learning the language needed to gain the content knowledge for high-stakes tests. Other lessons deal specifically with the language of the test and support targeted instruction on test items. The teaching strategies included in this book are varied and differentiated in order to meet the different needs of English language learners.

The appendix contains a list of academic language vocabulary compiled from a review of grades 9–11 assessments. These words are the academic English of literature, reading, writing, viewing, and representing, and the process/function vocabulary of test questions. The term *academic English* is based on Jim Cummins's theory of language proficiency, which states that there is a distinction between conversational and academic language (Cummins, 1983).

This manual draws from what the U.S. Department of Education calls professional wisdom: "the judgment that individuals acquire through experience" (Whitehurst, 2002). The foundation of solid professional wisdom can provide valuable insights into effective practice. We present this manual in the hope that it will support and assist teachers as they work to instruct the English language learners in their classrooms.

Chapter 1

Teaching the Language of the Reading-Objective Questions

Comparatives and Superlatives

The use of superlatives, especially irregular superlatives such as the word *best*, may be a source of confusion for English language learners. It is important to teach superlatives by first introducing the concept of comparatives. Using role-playing and board games when introducing comparatives and superlatives motivates students to learn and encourages them to practice the skill orally, which aids retention.

Implications for High-Stakes Testing

The grammatical structure of objective questions on the reading portion of standardized tests often includes the use of the irregular superlative word *best*. The test questions require students to determine the best answer to the question. If they do not understand the concept of superlatives, students are unable to choose the correct response.

Lesson Plan for Teaching Comparatives and Superlatives

Materials

- Transparency of "Best" Reading Questions handout (page 23)

- Blank paper, one sheet per student

- Copies of reading portion from a standardized test, one per pair or group

- Highlighters, one per pair or group

Academic Vocabulary

Understanding the meaning of the following terms is critical to a student's success in this lesson. It will not be possible—or practical—to teach all the words on this list at once, nor is this an exhaustive list of vocabulary that is necessary to know for this lesson. Also keep in mind that many students will already be familiar with many of these words.

adjective	object	suffix
comparative	quality	superlative
irregular	size	unique

Activities

1. Write the word *Comparatives* on the board. Pass out blank sheets of paper, and have students draw a simple object, such as a star, a tree, a flower, or a house. Students should all draw the same object. Do not give instructions about size, color, or detail.

2. After they have finished, ask the students (either as a class or in small groups) to line up according to the size of their objects. Have students line up in order from largest to smallest, from left to right (see figure 1.1).

Figure 1.1: This is a visual representation of step 2.

3. When the students are lined up in order, compare the objects by asking questions, encouraging the students to respond in full sentences using the language of the questions.

    Question: If John's star is big, what is Maria's star (to the left of John's)?

    Response: Maria's star is bigger than John's star.

    Question: If Spencer's star is small, what is Yolanda's star (to the right of Spencer's)?

    Response: Yolanda's star is smaller than Spencer's star.

4. Write the responses on the board, underlining the comparative suffix *-er*. Explain that the *-er* suffix means "more." Explain to the students that just as the class compared the sizes of their drawings, comparatives compare two things to each other. Write the words *bigger* and *smaller* under the word *Comparatives* on the board. Continue to ask questions, and allow students to respond using the comparative form, adding to the list of comparatives on the board. Possible responses may include the comparatives *prettier, nicer, cooler, larger, tinier,* and *cuter,* depending on the object drawn.

5. Now write the word *Superlatives* on the board next to the heading *Comparatives*. Explain that when something is unique because it has the most or least of a particular quality, the suffix *-est* is added to the end of the adjective describing it. Also, the word *the* is used before the adjective because it describes something that is one of a kind.

6. Now ask questions using superlatives, such as: **Who has the small<u>est</u> star? Who has the bigg<u>est</u> star?**

7. Write the responses to the questions on the board, underlining the suffix *-est*, such as: **Joe's star is the bigg<u>est</u>. Tommy's star is the small<u>est</u>.**

To the list of comparatives on the board, add the superlative forms of the words next to them, such as *biggest* and *smallest*.

8. Finally, write the word *best* under the column of words under the *Superlative* heading, and explain that the word *best* is also a superlative. Ask students what the comparative form of the word *best* would be (*better*), and write it next to the word *best* in the *Comparatives* column.

    It may also be necessary to explain to students that *best* is the superlative form of *good*. *Best* is an irregular superlative because the regular superlative form of *good* "should" be *goodest*. Ask students if any of them ever used the word *goodest* when they were first learning English, and praise them for understanding the use of the superlative suffix *–est*.

9. Now ask students: **Which student drew the BEST star?** Although students may have known the meaning of the word *best,* they were probably unaware that it is a superlative and that it means something that is better than anything else. Explain that just as with other superlatives, the word *best* always has the word *the* in front of it because it is the singular object with that quality. There is only one *best*.

10. Vote on the best drawing by having students raise their hands or applaud for their favorite. Give an award or certificate to the student who wins the most votes.

11. Discuss with the students what they have learned from this activity, asking questions such as: **Was it easy or difficult to choose one best drawing? Why? Were the other drawings good, too? Did everyone choose the same drawing? Did everyone agree on which drawing was the best? Does that mean the other drawings weren't good?**

12. Explain that just as it was difficult to vote on the best drawing, sometimes it is difficult to choose the best answer to a question. On standardized tests, the word *best* is used to indicate that although all the answers may be good, only one is the best. Discuss how students can determine which answer is the best by using strategies such as answering the question mentally before reading the responses, reading all the responses before choosing an answer, and going back into the passage to find evidence to support their choice.

13. Place a transparency of the "Best" Reading Questions handout (page 23) on the overhead (individual copies of the handout can be given to each student, if desired), and explain that the questions on the handout are all taken from the reading portions of standardized tests. Read through the questions with the students, and discuss the use of the superlative *best*.

14. Pair or group the students, and give each pair or group a copy of the reading portion of a standardized test and a highlighter. Have students search through the objective questions to find and highlight the word *best*.

15. As a class, read through the reading selections in the test, and work together to answer the first few best questions in the objective portion. Then allow the pairs or groups to work together to answer the rest. When all students have finished, share answers and discuss how students decided which ones were the best.

Spanish and English Cognates

What is a cognate? *Cognates* are words that are spelled (although not pronounced) identically or nearly identically in Spanish and English.

Table 1.1: Examples of Identical Cognates

English	Spanish
color	color
doctor	doctor
horrible	horrible
hospital	hospital
popular	popular

Table 1.2: Examples of Nearly Identical Cognates

English	Spanish
conversation	conversación
intelligent	inteligente
music	música
program	programa
violence	violencia

Cognates offer Spanish-speaking English language learners (ELLs) a wealth of words to add to their English vocabularies. While this concept may seem obvious to the teacher, ELLs do not usually notice it independently. In fact, many ELLs have a difficult time grasping exact cognates due to pronunciation differences. Because there are thousands of words in English with Latin roots, "making the cognate connection" is an important skill for English language learners.

Implications for High-Stakes Testing

For Spanish-speaking ELLs, recognizing cognates is a powerful tool for understanding the academic vocabulary on high-stakes tests. However, the key is that commonly used, high-frequency Spanish words have English cognates that are much more academic in nature. These English academic words are not used frequently in conversational English but do appear regularly in texts.

For example, *determinar* is a Spanish high-frequency word. The English cognate is *determine*. *Determine* is more likely to be found in the academic language used in a textbook. In conversation, English speakers would say *decide*. See table 1.3 for additional examples.

The term *realia* refers to real-life objects that can be used to improve student understanding of situations and concepts. Realia is an important part of helping ELL students recognize which words are similar in both languages.

Table 1.3: Additional Cognate Examples

Spanish	Academic English	Conversational English
amigable	amicable	friendly
colegas	colleagues	coworkers
determinar	determine	decide
elegir	elect	choose
encontrar	encounter	find
error	error	mistake
mandíbula	mandibule	jaw
olfato	olfaction	smell
significar	signify	mean
subterráneo	subterranean	underground
tarifa	tariff	fee
velocidad	velocity	speed

Lesson Plan for Spanish and English Cognates

Materials

- English and Spanish Cognates handouts, one per student (pages 24–30)

- Transparencies of The Cognate Restaurant and El Restaurante de los Cognados handouts (pages 31 and 32)

- False Cognates handout (pages 33–34), one per student

- Realia—cereal box, chocolate, banana, tea bag, coffee, tomato soup can

- Dictionaries, one per student

- Any English language arts (ELA) textbooks, one per student

- One newspaper or magazine per pair of students

- State or provincial assessment reading passage, one per pair

- Transparency of a selected passage from the ELA textbook

Academic Vocabulary

Understanding the meaning of the following terms is critical to a student's success in this lesson. It will not be possible—or practical—to teach all the words on this list at once, nor is this an exhaustive list of vocabulary that is necessary to know for this lesson. Also keep in mind that many students will already be familiar with many of these words.

cognate	newspaper	similar
identical	predict	suffix
magazine	prefix	variation
margin		

Activities

1. Tell students that they already have a tool that they can use to be better readers and writers of English. They have this tool because they are Spanish speakers.

2. Hold up the realia, piece by piece, and ask the students what each one is. Write the English and Spanish names of the items on the board or overhead as you hold them up (see El Restaurante de los Cognados on page 32). Ask students what they notice (that the words are the same or similar in each language).

3. Show a transparency of The Cognate Restaurant menu. Ask, "If your parents or someone you know who cannot speak any English saw this menu in a restaurant, would they be able to understand it?" Next, have them look at a transparency of the Spanish menu and compare the two. Ask students what they notice.

4. Explain to students that words with the same or similar spelling and also the same meaning are called cognates. There are more than 7,000 Spanish/English cognates. Once students learn how to "make the cognate connection," they will have a larger vocabulary and will be able to predict the meanings of many unknown words.

5. Brainstorm a list of cognates that students know (animals are a good topic for this; see table 1.4, page 10).

6. Provide each student with a copy of the English/Spanish Cognates handouts. Beginning with the nouns pages, explain to students the rules for changing word endings to create cognates. Depending on the pace of the class, the material can be covered at the rate of one part of speech per week or one ending per day.

7. Have students open their ELA textbooks to a familiar passage. Using a transparency of the passage, read through it with the students, stopping to identify and underline cognates. As cognates are found, write them on the board. Have students look the cognates up in the dictionary. Discuss the variations between English and Spanish in the spelling patterns of the prefixes and suffixes.

8. Have students pair up and read through newspaper or magazine articles and find cognates, underlining them and making a list on a separate piece of paper.

9. In the same pairs, have students read through a copy of a reading passage from a state or provincial assessment, underlining the cognates and writing the equivalent Spanish word in the margin. As a culminating activity, read through the passage with the students and identify the cognates, allowing students to modify their notations as needed. Help students understand the use of cognates to determine word meanings.

10. In these explorations, students may discover that some words that seem to be cognates do not mean the same thing. These words are known as *false cognates*. If students do not realize this concept, present examples to illustrate it. Explain that only one of every ten cognates is false. Give a copy of the False Cognates handout to each student.

Table 1.4: Animal Cognates

English	Spanish	English	Spanish
baboon	babuino	hyena	hiena
camel	camello	kangaroo	canguro
canary	canario	koala	koala
cat	gato	leopard	leopardo
chimpanzee	chimpancé	lion	león
dolphin	delfín	llama	llama
elephant	elefante	pelican	pelícano
giraffe	jirafa	penguin	pingüino
gorilla	gorila	rhinoceros	rinoceronte
hippopotamus	hipopótamo	tiger	tigre

Greek and Latin Roots and Affixes

Greek and Latin roots and affixes are used extensively in the English language. Students need to know these word parts to build vocabulary for comprehending more complex text and concepts.

Implications for High-Stakes Testing

Limited conceptual knowledge and difficulty in understanding word meanings can hinder English language learners' success on high-stakes exams. Understanding Greek and Latin roots and affixes will help students build vocabulary for comprehending more complex text and concepts.

Lesson Plan for Greek and Latin Roots and Affixes

Materials

- Greek and Latin Word Parts List handout (pages 35–38), one per student

- Most Common Word Parts in Printed School English handout (page 39), one per student

- Word Parts Activity handout (page 40), one per group

- Word Web handout (page 41), five copies per group

- Word Parts Scavenger Hunt handout (page 42), one per student

- Highlighters in two colors, one set per group

- Dictionaries, one per group

- English language arts (ELA) textbook, one per student

Academic Vocabulary

Understanding the meaning of the following terms is critical to a student's success in this lesson. It will not be possible—or practical—to teach all the words on this list at once, nor is this an exhaustive list of vocabulary that is necessary to know for this lesson. Keep in mind that many students will already be familiar with many of these words.

affix	frequent	scavenger hunt
base word	glossary	similar
boldface	predict	suffix
context	prefix	web
definition	root	

Activities

1. Write a word, such as *tricycle*, on the board. Ask students what other words they know that sound similar to this word or that have the same word parts. For example, students might say *trilingual, bicycle, unicycle, trident, tripod,* and so on. (If students are beginning English speakers, the teacher may have to provide other words.) Ask what these words have in common (they all contain *tri-* or *-cycle*). Ask students if they know what any of these words mean. Once a few answers are given, ask again what the words have in common. Explain that a *prefix* is a small word part that goes at the beginning of a word. A *root* is a base whose meaning is changed by adding a prefix. Explain that *tri-* is a prefix that means *three*. The root *-cycle* means *round* or *wheel*, so *tricycle* means something with three wheels. In the word *tripod, tri-* is the prefix. There is no root word part, but there is a suffix. The suffix is *-pod* and means *foot*. Explain that a *suffix* is a small word part that goes at the end of a word. Then ask students what the other words might mean.

2.   Give each student a copy of the Greek and Latin Word Parts List handout, and discuss it with them. Point out that the most frequently used word parts are in boldface. It may be helpful to discuss these with the students, using the Most Common Word Parts in Printed School English handout (page 39).

3.   Form groups of no more than four students. Give each group a copy of the Word Parts Activity handout, designed to help them think about how word parts can help determine meaning, along with set of highlighters. Tell each group to highlight the affixes (prefixes and/or suffixes) in one color and the root or base word in a different color. Ask students to explain their answers to the class.

4.   Once all groups have shared, give each group five copies of the Word Web handout and one dictionary. Then assign five specific word parts from the Greek and Latin Word Parts List handout to each group. Ask students to find words containing their assigned word parts as well as the definitions for these words. Together construct a Word Web for the affix *min* (see figure 1.2).

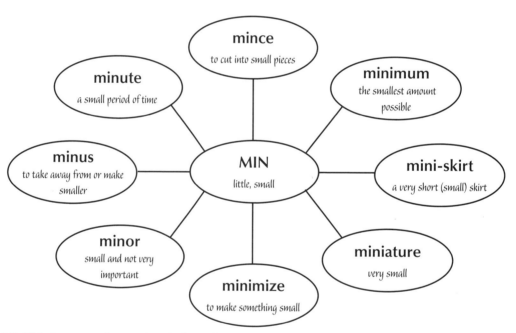

Figure 1.2: This is a sample word web for *min*.

5.   Next, have students complete a scavenger hunt for words in their ELA textbook. Give students the Word Parts Scavenger Hunt handout. Write a limited number of word parts on the board. Ask students to find a word that contains one of the Greek or Latin word parts listed and note the context in which it is used. Also ask students to predict a definition and then look up the word in the textbook glossary to confirm the definition.

Multiple-Meaning Words

One of the most difficult aspects of the English language is that it contains many words that can have multiple meanings and can also be used as different parts of speech. These words often appear in multiple contexts. Students must be able to determine meaning in order to successfully negotiate the understanding of concepts in various contexts.

Implications for High-Stakes Testing

To fully understand the concepts being assessed, students must have strategies to determine the contextually appropriate meaning for multiple-meaning words.

Lesson Plan for Multiple-Meaning Words

Materials

- Blank paper, two sheets per student

- Markers, one set per student

- Stapler

- Multiple-Meaning Words Chart handout, one per student (page 43)

Academic Vocabulary

Understanding the meaning of the following terms is critical to a student's success in this lesson. It will not be possible—or practical—to teach all the words on this list at once, nor is this an exhaustive list of vocabulary that is necessary to know for this lesson. Also keep in mind that many students will already be familiar with many of these words.

appropriate	flap	part of speech
bottom	flip book	represent
context	meaning	section
definition	multiple	sentence
edge		

Activities

1. Write the following statements on the board. Ask students to do a think-pair-share to discuss how the meaning of the word *cool* differs in each sentence.

   The fan will cool me off. The new football stadium is cool!

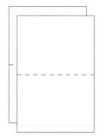

Figure 1.4

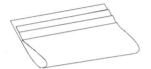

Figure 1.5

Table

Figure 1.6

Table

(noun) A piece of furniture

Figure 1.7

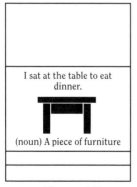

I sat at the table to eat dinner.

(noun) A piece of furniture

Figure 1.8

2. Explain that words in English can have multiple meanings and can also be used as different parts of speech when used in different contexts. It is important to consider the context of a word before deciding on a meaning.

3. Give students two sheets of blank paper. Have them place their top sheet of paper one inch above the bottom edge of the second sheet (see figure 1.4).

4. Fold the set of papers so that the top sheet is one inch above its bottom edge (see figure 1.5). This will create a flip book. Staple the book along the fold.

5. On the top flap, ask students to write the word *table* (see figure 1.6). Explain that *table* is a word in English that has multiple meanings.

6. On the second flap, on the bottom edge, ask students to write the part of speech (noun). Ask them to write the following definition: **A piece of furniture** (see figure 1.7).

7. Raise the top flap and ask the students to draw a picture of a table on this section. Ask them to write the following sentence (or a sentence of their own creation) on the top of the page: **I sat at the table to eat dinner** (see figure 1.8).

8. On the third flap, on the next edge, ask students to write the part of speech (noun) and a second definition of the word *table*: **A list of numbers, facts, or information arranged in rows across and down a page.** As before, ask students to draw a picture representing this definition and write the following sentence (or a sentence of their own creation): **The table shows the amount of rain that fell during each month** (see figure 1.9).

9. On the last flap, on the bottom edge, ask students to write the part of speech (verb) and a third definition of the word *table*: **To decide to deal with an offer or idea at a later time.** Once again, ask students to draw a picture representing this definition and write the following sentence (or a sentence of their own creation): **The committee decided to table the discussion when it could not agree on a solution to the problem** (see figure 1.10).

10. Ask students to think of times and contexts when these words might be used. Explain that a flip book can be used to help learn vocabulary and determine which definition is appropriate for different contexts.

11. Repeat this strategy for additional multiple-meaning words. Students can use the Multiple-Meaning Words Chart handout to compile a list of multiple-meaning words they encounter through instruction or their own reading. Some multiple-meaning words that can be used for instruction include those in table 1.5.

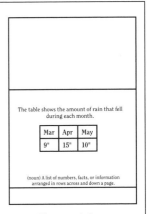

The table shows the amount of rain that fell during each month.

Mar	Apr	May
9"	15"	10"

(noun) A list of numbers, facts, or information arranged in rows across and down a page.

Figure 1.9

Table 1.5: Examples of Multiple-Meaning Words

account	cell	field	rate	stock
act	cover	land	scale	table
bank	draft	pass	set	wave
bill	draw	place	solution	web
capital	fault	plant	state	

Table

(noun) A piece of furniture

(noun) A list of numbers, facts, or information arranged in rows across and down a page.

(verb) To decide to deal with an offer or idea at a later time.

Figure 1.10

Teen Advice Columns Using *Could, Should,* and *Would*

The words *could, should,* and *would* are English words that are spelled using the same pattern but have vastly different meanings. They are part of a text structure common in test questions and also the conversational language of native English speakers. However, they may not be well-known to English language learners because they represent more advanced verb types and tenses that students may not have been taught. *Should* is a modal verb, and *could* and *would* are most often used in test questions as the conditional tense of the verb *to be*.

Implications for High-Stakes Testing

Many questions on standardized English language arts tests, especially on the revising and editing portions, contain the words *could, should,* and *would*, which must be understood in order for students to choose the correct answer. Students unfamiliar with this question structure may be unable to determine the meaning of the question or the response containing the word.

Lesson Plan for Teen Advice Columns Using
Could, Should, and Would

Materials

- Advice columns, such as *Dear Abby*, from teen magazines or newspapers

- Teenage Problems handout (pages 44–45), one per group

- Advice Columns Answer Sheet handout (page 46), one per group

- Copies of English language arts portion from a standardized test, one per group

- Highlighters, one per group

Academic Vocabulary

Understanding the meaning of the following terms is critical to a student's success in this lesson. It will not be possible—or practical—to teach all the words on this list at once, nor is this an exhaustive list of vocabulary that is necessary to know for this lesson. Also keep in mind that many students will already be familiar with many of these words.

advice	magazine	should
column	newspaper	teen
could	possibly	teenager
definitely	problem	would

Activities

Using authentic literature such as newspapers and magazines is a good way to incorporate realia into a lesson. The school newspaper may even have an advice column.

1. Ask students if they have ever read the advice columns in magazines or newspapers. Show them examples of some advice columns, and explain what they are if students are not familiar with the genre.

2. Discuss what types of problems teenagers might have that would prompt them to write to a columnist for advice. Ask the students if they have ever written for advice, or what they would ask about if they did.

3. Read one of the problems, such as the following example, to the students, allowing them to discuss the problem as a class and give their ideas for advice.

Dear Advice Column,

My family has money problems. They need me to get a job and help pay for things. I want to get a job and make some money, and I do want to help my family, but my dad wants me to give him all the money that I make. I don't think that is fair. I think I should get to keep some of the money because I will be doing the work. I want to save up for a car and some other things for myself, like new clothes, so that my dad won't have to pay for them. My dad has a bad temper, though, and I am afraid of making him mad. How can I get him to understand that I want to give him some of my money and keep some of it, too?

Sincerely,
Tommy, 16

4. Write the following questions across the top of the board, underlining the words *should*, *would*, and *could*:

What <u>should</u> the person (definitely) do?

What <u>would</u> happen if the person were to do that?

What else <u>could</u> the person (possibly) do?

5. Explain the definitions of *should*, *would*, and *could* in simple English as follows: **Should is used when giving advice about definitely doing something. Would is used when talking about something expected to happen. (In the case of giving advice, it is what will happen after the person takes the advice.) Could is used to suggest possibly doing something.**

6. Ask the class the first question and allow many students to respond. Have them discuss all the different advice and the possible outcomes. On the board, under the first question, write the students' advice to the person in the example problem. Typical responses might be: **He should get a job. He should tell his father that he got a job. He should talk to his father and explain that he is trying to save him money by paying for his own things. He should write down all the reasons why it is fair for him to keep some of the money he makes and give the list to his father. He should ask his mother to talk to his father for him.**

7. Next, ask the students what they expect to happen if Tommy takes the advice they have given. Show them the second question: What *would* happen if the person were to do that? Allow students to discuss the possibilities and record their answers on the board under the second question. Typical responses might be: **He would make enough money to help his family and also to save some. His mom would be able to help him talk to his father, so his father would understand. The list would explain things to his father without his father getting mad.**

8. Finally, ask students the third question: What else *could* the person do? Let students brainstorm about other possibilities that might be different from the advice they would get from a professional advice columnist. Record their answers on the board under the third question. Typical responses might be: **He could get a job and not tell his father. He could get two jobs and keep the money from one of them. He could move and live with somebody else.**

9. Place students in four small groups, and give each group copies of the Teenage Problems handout and the Advice Columns Answer Sheet handout. Explain to students that they will be assigned one of the teen problems from the handout, and their group is to read through the problem, discuss it, and fill in their answers on the Advice Columns Answer Sheet handout. Ask students to use the words *should, would,* or *could* in their answers and to use complete sentences. A reporter from each group can use the handout to report the group's responses back to the class.

10. After students have become familiar with the meanings of the words *should, would,* and *could,* pair or group them and give each set of students a copy of the English language arts portion from a standardized test and highlighters. Have students search through the questions and responses to find and highlight the words *should, would,* and *could.*

11. As a class, read through the selections in the test and work together to answer a few of the questions containing the highlighted words. Then allow the pairs or groups to work together to answer the rest. When all students have finished, share answers and discuss.

Suggestion

- To reinforce learning, ask students to write about a problem they have had. Students should not write any names, including their own, on their problem descriptions. Specify that length should be from one paragraph to one-half page long only. After previewing the problem descriptions and checking for appropriateness, distribute the problems to other students. Have students answer the questions about the problem on an Advice Columns Answer Sheet handout. Ask students to share their responses with the class, or have students exchange and share with a partner.

Reading Test Question Stems in Classroom Discussion

It is important to help students realize that as they read, they should be questioning what they are reading because "a reader with no questions might just as well abandon the book" (Harvey & Goudvis, 2000, p. 82). In this lesson, structured support is provided for students in the form of question-stem sentence frames from the reading portion of standardized tests. Using question stems containing academic language enables students to internalize that language through discussions with their teacher and with other students.

Implications for High-Stakes Testing

Even though English language learners may be able to comprehend the reading passage on a standardized test, their understanding may be limited by the question format. When teachers use the reading question stems in guided reading, read alouds, and class discussions, students become familiar with the format as well as the academic language of the test.

Lesson Plan for Reading Test Question Stems in Classroom Discussion

Materials

- Mix and Mingle Instructions (page 47) to be used on the overhead or written on the board

- Reading Question Stem Chart handout (pages 48–49), one per student

- Reading Question Stem Cards (pages 50–54), copied on cardstock, cut apart, laminated if desired, and placed on a metal ring, one set per student

- Reading Question Stem Strips (pages 55–65), copied on cardstock, cut apart, laminated if desired, one set per student

Academic Vocabulary

Understanding the meaning of the following terms is critical to a student's success in this lesson. It will not be possible—or practical—to teach all the words on this list at once, nor is this an exhaustive list of vocabulary that is necessary to know for this lesson. Also keep in mind that many students will already be familiar with many of these words.

affect	entry	means
allow	establish	mostly

appropriate	explain	primarily
best	express	relate
cite	face (verb)	respond
conclude	following	reveal
contribute	imply	selection
convey	in order to	serve
demonstrate	indicate	show
describe	intend	significance
develop	mainly	stem (verb)
disclose	match	suggest
element	meaning	support
emphasize		

Activities

It is not essential to copy, laminate, and assemble the Reading Question Stem Strips. However, doing this creates a sturdy manipulative set that can be used over and over again as a class set. It is recommended that teachers create a class set of the manipulative cards rather than a set of cards for each individual student.

1. Explicitly teach the academic vocabulary in the Reading Question Stem Strips, which are the process/function words found most frequently in the questions. (It is assumed that the academic vocabulary of the reading concepts, such as *main idea, theme, setting*, and so on, are being explicitly taught in other lessons.)

2. Give each student a copy of the Reading Question Stem Chart handout. In addition, a large poster of the chart can be made and placed in an easily visible part of the room.

3. Familiarize the students with the organization of the question stems by showing them how the questions are organized according to concepts. Point out the individual concepts, which are the headings at the top of each section, such as Main Idea, Setting, and Plot Development. Explain that the wording of the question stems under each concept is similar to the wording on the reading portion of the standardized test they will be taking.

4. Explain to students that when they are talking about passages or stories they have read in class, use the question stems from the charts to facilitate their discussions. Demonstrate how to turn the stems into interrogatives by placing the words *who, what, when, where, which, how,* or *why* at the beginning of the question stem, along with the verb *is* or *are.* (The interrogative form of the question stem can be found on the Reading Question Stem Strips.)

Question stem: This selection is mainly about _____.

Interrogative version: What is this selection mainly about?

> Main Idea and Supporting Details
>
> ## What is paragraph ___ mostly/mainly about?

Question stem: The theme in this story is best revealed through _____.

Interrogative version: How is the theme in this story best revealed?

> Theme
>
> ## How is the theme in this story best revealed?

Although it is important for the students to be able to understand how to turn the question stems into interrogative versions, it is more important that they understand the meaning of the stems because that is the form that will appear on the test.

5. Model the use of the stems by reviewing a story the students have already read. A familiar fairy tale, such as *Cinderella*, could be used for this purpose. Begin a discussion of the story by asking questions using the stems from the charts, defining the process/function words in simple English. Ask, **What do the actions of the stepsisters disclose [or make us know]? What is one conflict that Cinderella faces [or has to deal with]? In this story, what does the glass slipper symbolize [or stand for]?**

Show the students how to fill in the blanks in the question stems with the names of the characters or items from the story and then how to formulate their answers using the same stem. The actions of the stepsisters disclose that _____. One conflict that Cinderella faces is _____. In this story, the glass slipper symbolizes _____.

Point out to students which question stems are being used for the discussion. Explain to them that they are now "speaking" the academic language of the test.

6.   After the question stems have been introduced and modeled, insist that students use them when interacting in class.

Suggestions

- Allow students to read a selection together in small groups, and assign each group a particular number of questions from each Reading Question Stem Card to discuss. For example, the teacher may assign a group one question stem from each card. Members choose one question from their question stem card sets and then ask and answer their own question. The students take turns asking and answering a question until the required number and type of questions have been discussed.

- After placing students in small groups, assign one of the Reading Question Stem Cards containing one or two concepts to each group, and ask group members to discuss all the questions on that card. A reporter from each group reports the discussion findings to the class.

- Using the Reading Question Stem Strips, play Mix and Mingle as a review activity. Allow students to draw one question strip out of a bag, hand the strips out to them randomly, or assign question strips to students ahead of time. Instruct students to find a partner, or assign partners. Tell students that they are to compliment one thing about their partner (at this point, it may be appropriate to give a mini-lesson on what a compliment is and how to give one) and then read and answer the question on their strip. Then the second partner compliments the first partner and reads and answers his or her question. Then partners exchange questions, find a new partner, and repeat the process a specific number of times. The instructions for the activity can be placed on the overhead or written on the board (see Mix and Mingle Instructions on page 47). After a sufficient number of questions have been asked and answered by the students, have them return to their seats and hold a class discussion using the questions they have already answered. This strategy scaffolds English language learners by allowing them to hear the answers to many questions in English before being asked to discuss the questions as a group.

- Allow students to take turns being the teacher and to ask questions of the class during discussions.

"Best" Reading Questions

- Which statement **best** supports the idea that _____?

- What is the **best** summary of paragraph(s) _____–_____?

- What is the **best** summary of the selection?

- Which line **best** summarizes a theme of the story?

- How is the theme in this story **best** revealed?

- How is the theme **best** demonstrated?

- Which sentence from the selection **best** helps the reader understand the author's feelings about the setting?

- Which sentence from the story **best** conveys _____?

- How is _____'s character **best** revealed?

- Which line from the story **best** reveals _____?

- Which quotation from the selection **best** summarizes the author's view?

- Which quotation from paragraph _____ **best** supports the generalization that _____?

- The author **best** develops this story by _____
_____.

English and Spanish Cognates: Nouns

Many English nouns should be instantly recognizable to a Spanish-speaking reader. With only slight modifications, usually a change to the word ending, many English nouns can easily be converted into Spanish nouns.

English nouns ending with *-or* are very often identical in Spanish.

-or = -or	
English	**Spanish**
actor →	actor
color →	color
error →	error
favor →	favor
tutor →	tutor

English nouns ending with *-al* are very often identical in Spanish.

-al = -al	
English	**Spanish**
animal →	animal
capital →	capital
hospital →	hospital
metal →	metal
moral →	moral

Many English nouns ending with *-ist* can be converted into Spanish nouns by adding *-a* to the end of the word.

-ist = -ista	
English	**Spanish**
artist →	artista
dentist →	dentista
novelist →	novelista
optimist →	optimista
pianist →	pianista

Many English nouns ending with *-ism* can be converted into Spanish nouns by adding *-o* to the end of the word.

-ism = -ismo	
English	**Spanish**
idealism →	idealismo
optimism →	optimismo
organism →	organismo
racism →	racismo
realism →	realismo

continued

English and Spanish Cognates: Nouns (continued)

Many English nouns ending with *-nce* can be converted into Spanish nouns by changing the *e* at the end of the word to *ia*.

-ncia = -nce		
English		**Spanish**
correspondence	→	correspondencia
distance	→	distancia
experience	→	experiencia
influence	→	influencia
presence	→	presencia

Many English nouns ending with *-ty* can be converted into Spanish nouns by changing *-ty* to *-dad*.

-ty = -dad		
English		**Spanish**
capacity	→	capacidad
electricity	→	electricidad
society	→	sociedad
university	→	universidad
variety	→	variedad

English and Spanish Cognates: Adjectives

Many English adjectives can be converted into Spanish simply by changing the word ending. Almost all Spanish adjectives are either masculine (ending in *o*) or feminine (ending in *a*). An adjective's gender is usually dictated by the gender of the noun to which it refers.

English adjectives ending with *-al* are very often identical in Spanish.

-al = -al	
English	**Spanish**
final →	final
local →	local
natural →	natural
normal →	normal
usual →	usual

Many English adjectives ending with *-ble* are very often identical in Spanish.

-ble = -ble	
English	**Spanish**
horrible →	horrible
notable →	notable
probable →	probable
terrible →	terrible

Many English adjectives ending with *-ic* can be converted into Spanish adjectives by adding *-o* to the end of the word.

-ic = -ico	
English	**Spanish**
artistic →	artístico
automatic →	automático
electric →	eléctrico
fantastic →	fantástico
romantic →	romántico

Many English adjectives ending with *-nt* can be converted into Spanish adjectives by adding *-e* to the end of the word.

-nt = -nte	
English	**Spanish**
convenient →	conveniente
ignorant →	ignorante
important →	importante
permanent →	permanente

continued

English and Spanish Cognates: Adjectives (continued)

Many English adjectives ending with *-ive* can be converted into Spanish adjectives by changing *-e* at the end of the word to *-o*.

-ive = -ivo	
English	**Spanish**
active	→ activo
creative	→ creativo
definitive	→ definitivo
negative	→ negativo
positive	→ positivo

Many English adjectives ending with *-ous* can be converted into Spanish nouns by changing *-ous* at the end of the word to *-oso*.

-ous = -oso	
English	**Spanish**
curious	→ curioso
delicious	→ delicioso
famous	→ famoso
generous	→ generoso
glorious	→ glorioso

Many English adjectives ending with *-ile* can be converted into Spanish adjectives by removing *-e* at the end of the word.

-ile = -il	
English	**Spanish**
fertile	→ fértil
fragile	→ frágil
hostile	→ hostil
juvenile	→ juvenil

Many English adjectives ending with *-ary* can be converted into Spanish adjectives by changing *-y* at the end of the word to *-io*.

-ary = -ario	
English	**Spanish**
legendary	→ legendario
literary	→ literario
ordinary	→ ordinario
secondary	→ secondario
voluntary	→ voluntario

Many English adjectives ending with *-id* can be converted into Spanish adjectives by adding *-o* to the end of the word.

-id = -ido	
English	**Spanish**
intrepid	→ intrépido
rapid	→ rápido
solid	→ sólido

-id = -ido	
English	**Spanish**
splendid	→ espléndido
valid	→ válido

English and Spanish Cognates: Verbs

There are many English verbs that can be converted into Spanish, usually by changing the ending of the English verb and adding -ar, -er, or -ir.

Almost every English infinitive verb ending with -ate (celebrate) can be converted into a Spanish infinitive verb by replacing the final -ate with -ar (celebrar).

-ate = -ar		
English		**Spanish**
calculate	→	calcular
concentrate	→	concentrar
create	→	crear
demonstrate	→	demostrar
estimate	→	estimar
exaggerate	→	exagerar
negotiate	→	negociar
operate	→	operar
participate	→	participar
terminate	→	terminar

Many English infinitive verbs of more than one syllable ending with VOWEL + CONSONANT + e (examine) can be converted into Spanish infinitive verbs by dropping the final -e and adding -ar (examinar).

-VC + e = -VC + ar		
English		**Spanish**
accuse	→	acusar
adore	→	adorar
authorize	→	authorizer
complete	→	completar
converse	→	conversar

Almost every English infinitive verb ending with -ify (signify) can be converted into a Spanish infinitive verb by replacing the final -ify with -ificar (significar).

-ify = -ificar		
English		**Spanish**
amplify	→	amplificar
certify	→	certificar
gratify	→	gratificar
justify	→	justificar
modify	→	modificar
notify	→	notificar
pacify	→	pacificar
simplify	→	simplificar
solidify	→	solidificar
unify	→	unificar

Many English infinitive verbs ending with VOWEL + CONSONANT + t (result) can be converted into Spanish infinitive verbs by adding -ar, -er, or -ir to the end of the English verb (resultar).

-VC + t = -ar, -er, -ir		
English		**Spanish**
consult	→	consultar
insult	→	insultar
present	→	presentar

continued

English and Spanish Cognates: Verbs (continued)

-VC + e = -VC + ar	
English	**Spanish**
escape →	escapar
ignore →	ignorar
imagine →	imaginar
invite →	invitar
organize →	organizar
prepare →	preparar
utilize →	utilizar

-VC + t = -ar, -er, -ir	
English	**Spanish**
convert →	convertir
export →	exportar
import →	importar
insist →	insistir
represent →	representar

English and Spanish Cognates: Adverbs

In Spanish, *-mente* combines with feminine adjectives to form adverbs. In English, *-ly* combines with many adjectives to form adverbs.

Many English adverbs ending with *-ly* can be converted into Spanish adverbs by changing the *-ly* at the end of the word to *-mente*.

Adjective		Adverb	
English	**Spanish**	**English**	**Spanish**
absolute → absoluta		absolutely → absolutamente	
complete → completa		completely → completamente	
evident → evidente		evidently → evidentemente	
exact → exacta		exactly → exactamente	
final → final		finally → finalmente	
natural → natural		naturally → naturalmente	
normal → normal		normally → normalmente	
probable → probable		probably → probablemente	

The Cognate Restaurant

Breakfast

Cereal

Toast

Banana

Coffee

Tea

Lunch

Sandwich

Fruit Salad

Tomato Soup

Soda

Dinner

Steak

Potato

Salad

Cauliflower

Chocolate Tart

El Restaurante de los Cognados

Desayuno

Cereal

Pan tostado

Banana

Café

Té

Almuerzo

Sandwich

Ensalada de fruta

Sopa de tomate

Soda

Cena

Bistec

Patata

Ensalada

Coliflor

Tarta de chocolate

False Cognates

English Word	English Meaning	Spanish Word	Spanish Meaning
actual	real	actual	current, at the present time
assist	help	asistir	to attend
attend	be present	atender	to take care of
billion	1,000,000,000	billón	1,000,000,000,000
bizarre	weird	bizarro	brave
body	physique	boda	wedding
camp	outdoor site	campo	field or countryside
carpet	rug	carpeta	file folder
complexion	coloring of the face	complexión	physiological build
compromise	settle	compromiso	promise or obligation
contest	challenge	contestar	to answer
deception	trickery	decepción	disappointment
delight	enjoyment	delito	crime
disgrace	dishonor	desgracia	mistake
embarrassed	humiliated	embarazada	pregnant
exit	outlet	éxito	hit or success
fabric	cloth	fábrica	factory
football	American game	fútbol	soccer
gang	group	ganga	bargain
large	big	largo	long
once	one time	once	eleven
pretend	fake	pretender	to try
record	write down	recordar	to remember

continued

False Cognates (continued)

English Word	English Meaning	Spanish Word	Spanish Meaning
rope	cord	ropa	clothing
revolver	gun	revolver	to stir
sensible	realistic	sensible	sensitive
soap	cleansing agent	sopa	soup
success	accomplishment	suceso	event or happening
tuna	fish	tuna	cactus or glee club

Greek and Latin Word Parts List

a-, an-	without		calidi-	hot
ab-	away from		cap-	take, hold
acri-	sharp		cata-	down, across, under
ad-	to, toward, near		ceno-	new
alieni-	another's		centi-	100
allo-	other, different		chron-	time
ambi-	both		circuli-	round
ana-	up, against		circum-	around
ante-	before, in front of		co-	together
anthrop-	human		con-	with
ant-, anti-	against, opposite, opposing		contra-	against
			-crat, -cracy	power, rule
apo-	away from		cred-	believe
aqua-	water		cryo-	cold
archeo-	old		crypto-	hidden
aster-, astro-	star		cyclo-	round
aud-	hear, listen to		de-	away, off
auto-	self, same		deca-	10
bary-	heavy		dem-	people
bene-	good		derm-	skin
bi-, bis-	twice, double		dexio, dextri-	right
biblio-	book		di-	two, twice, double
bio-, bi-	life, living organism		dia-	through
boni-	good		**dict-**	to say
brachy-	short		dis-	not, not, any
brevi-	brief		dis-	apart, removed

continued

Greek and Latin Word Parts List (continued)

dodeca-	12	gyro-	round
duc-	to lead, take	hemi-	half
dulci-	sweet	hepta-	7
dys-	hard, difficult, bad	hetero-	different
ex- (Latin)	out of	hex-, hexa-	6
ex- (Greek)	out of	holo-	entirely
ecto-	outside	homo-	alike, same
en-	in	humidi-	wet
endo-	within	hydr-, hydro-	water, liquid
ennea-	9	hyper-	excessive, over, above
epi-	on, upon		
equi-	equal	hypo-	below, under, bottom
eu-	easy, good, well		
exo-	outside, outward	identi-	same
extra-	outside, in addition to	idio-	one's own
		in-	in, into, on
fac-	make, do	in-	not, beyond belief
fort-	strong	infra-	below
gam-	united	inter-	between, among
gen-	race, birth, type	intro-	within
geo-	earth, geography	intus-	within
gylcol-	sweet	-ism	the study or theory of
-gram, -graph	written, record, drawn		
gravi-	heavy	iso-	equal
-gress	to walk	-ist	person
		-ject	to throw

continued

Greek and Latin Word Parts List (continued)

lati-	wide	novi-	new
lepto-	thin	octo-	8
-logue, -log	speech, to speak	-oid	like, resembling
-logy	expression, study	oligo-	few
longi-	long	opistho-	behind
macro-	large	oxy-	sharp
magni-	big	pachy-	thick
man-, manu-	hand	paleo-	old
mal-	bad	palin-	again
medio-	middle	pan-	all
mega-	big	para-	alongside of, beside
meso-	middle	path-	feeling, suffering
met-, miss-	send, sent	ped-, pod-	foot
meta-	with, after, beyond	**-ped(e), -pod**	foot
-meter, -metry	measuring device, measure	**pedo-, ped-**	child, children
micro-	small, little	pend-	to hang
milli-	1000	penta-	5
min-	small, little	per-	through, complete
mis-, mit-	wrongly, incorrect	peri-	around, near
miso-	hatred	-phile	loves, lover of
molli-	soft	philo-, phil-	strong love for
mono-	one, single	-phobe, -phobia	fear of a thing
morph-	form	**phon-**	sound
multi-	many	-phone	sound
neo-	new, recent	picro-	bitter
non-	not	poly-	many
		port-	to carry

continued

Greek and Latin Word Parts List (continued)

post-	after, behind	sub-	under, below
pre-	in front of, before	**struct-**	build, form
pro-	in front of, before	super-, supra-	above, upper
proso-	onward, in front	syn-	with
proto	front	tele-	far
psych-	mind	tenu-	thin
pseudo-	false	tetra-	4
quadrati-	square	therm-	heat
quadric-	4	thermo-	hot
re-	again, back, backward	tract-	to pull, drag
		trans-	across, through
retro-	backward	tri-	3
scaio-	left	ultra-	beyond
sclero-	hard	uni-	1
-scope	sight	vacuo-	empty
scrib-, script-	to write	validi-	strong
semi-	½	vario-	different
seni-	old	vert-	to turn
sesqui-	1½	via-, vis-	see
sicci-	dry	voc-	call
simili-	alike	xero-	dry
spec(t)-	look	zo-	animal
steno-	narrow		

Most Common Word Parts in Printed School English

Root	Meaning	Origin	Examples
aud	hear	Latin	audiophile, auditorium, audition
astro	star	Greek	astrology, astronaut, astronomy
bio	life	Greek	biography, biology
dict	speak, tell	Latin	dictate, predict, dictator
geo	earth	Greek	geology, geography
meter	measure	Greek	thermometer, barometer
min	little, small	Latin	minimum, minimal
mit, mis	send	Latin	mission, transmit, remit, missile
ped	foot	Latin	pedestrian, pedal, pedestal
phon	sound	Greek	phonograph, microphone, phoneme
port	carry	Latin	transport, portable, import
scrib, script	write	Latin	scribble, manuscript, inscription
spect	see	Latin	inspect, spectator, respect
struct	build, form	Latin	construction, destruction, instruct

Word Web

Name: _____ Date: _____

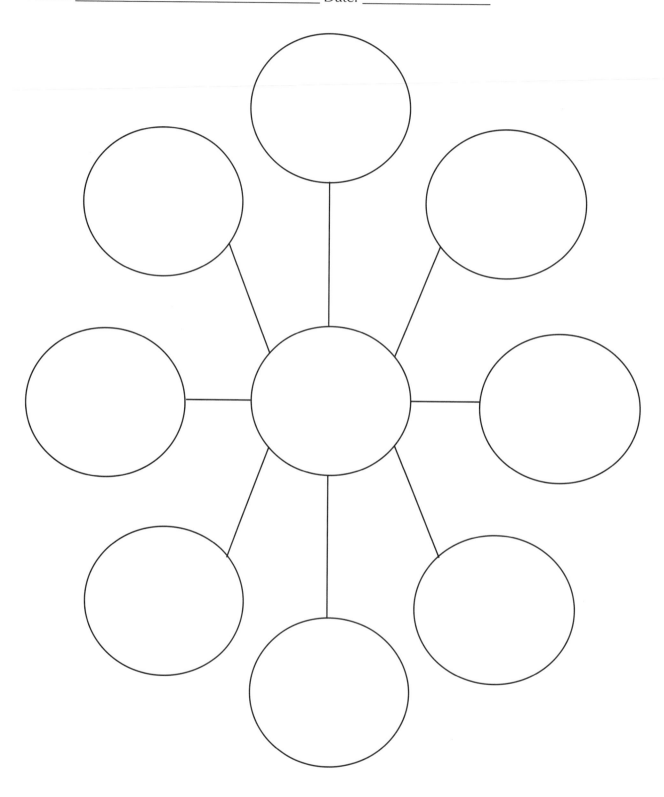

Word Parts Activity

Name: _____ Date: _____

1. Why is a *microscope* called a microscope?

2. How does a *microscope* differ from a *telescope*?

3. How does a *telephone* differ from a *telegram*?

4. What is the purpose of *antifreeze* in an automobile engine?

5. What happens if something *malfunctions*?

6. What is the difference between a *postdated* check and an *antedated* check?

7. If *a-* means without, what does *apolitical* mean?

8. If *biology* is the study of life, what is *anthropology*?

9. What is *astrology*?

10. What is a *philanthropist*?

11. What word means the study of animals?

12. If *geo-* means earth, what does *geology* mean?

13. If you have an *auditory* problem, what kind of problem do you have?

14. What do the word parts in *democracy* mean?

15. If you *contradict* someone's hypothesis, what are you doing?

16. Would you like to be called a *bibliophile*? Why or why not?

17. If you did not know what *manufacture* means, how could you figure it out?

18. If *credible* means believable, what does *incredible* mean?

19. What root do *pedal* and *pedestrian* have in common, and what does it mean?

20. When you give *credence* to someone's story, what are you doing?

21. If *tri-* means three, what is a *tripod*?

Word Parts Scavenger Hunt

Name: _____

Date: _____

Word Part	Word From Textbook	Context in Which Word Is Used	Predicted Definition	Glossary Definition

Multiple-Meaning Words Chart

Name: _____

Date: _____

Word	Definition 1	Definition 2	Definition 3

Teen Problems

Read through your problem with your group, and then answer the following questions on the Advice Columns Answer Sheet:

- What *should* the person (definitely) do?

- What *would* happen if the person were to do that?

- What else *could* the person (possibly) do?

Share your advice with the rest of the class.

Problem #1

Should I Marry Him?

I have been with my boyfriend for four years now, ever since I was in eighth grade. He wants to get married next year, but there are a couple of problems I have. One is the fact that I will still be in high school. He graduates this year, but I will be in 12th grade next year. I want to graduate, but he wants to have a baby right away. Another problem is that he doesn't have a job because he got hurt on his last job and can't work right now. I have a good job working at my uncle's restaurant and I make very good money. If I quit school and quit my job to get married and have a baby, I don't know how we would support ourselves. The last problem is that we would have to live with his family at first because we don't have enough money to get our own house. I love my boyfriend very much. He is very good to me. He is telling me that if I don't marry him now, I might lose him. I don't want to lose him. What should I do?

Sincerely,

Lara, 16

Problem #2

Should I Tell Her I Love Her?

I have a problem with my best friend. You see, I am a guy and she is a girl, and what she doesn't know is that I'm in love with her. I have had a crush on other girls before, but this is really different. We are very close, and I know that she likes me very much. We've known each other for about three years, and our friendship has constantly become better. We fight some-times, but we always make up. We meet almost every day and talk every day. We tell each other everything, so I know she is having problems with her boyfriend (who I think is no good for her). My problem is that I want to tell her I love her, but I don't want to ruin our friendship. We always have very much fun together. I'm afraid if I tell her I love her, she will not return the feelings and then our friendship will be ruined. On the other hand, I feel sometimes like my heart will break if I don't tell her. What if she feels the same way and is afraid to tell me? What should I do?

Sincerely,

Manny, 15

continued

Teen Problems (continued)

Problem #3

Please Help Me and My Family

My family doesn't get along. It's like we all hate each other. My mom, me, my two brothers, and a sister all live together. I am the oldest. We each have different problems. My mom wants to quit smoking, so she is really stressed out. I am really selfish (I just can't help it). One of my brothers is too bossy. He thinks that he is better than the rest of us and that he is the only one who helps my mom. My other brother is kind of depressed. He always starts fights and he's really spoiled (my mom doesn't yell at him for doing things wrong because he's so sad all the time, but when she does, he laughs at her). My sister (who's 7 years old) makes messes and doesn't clean them up. I really want to help because I don't like being upset all the time and having everyone hate everyone else. Even when we start to get along, someone will say something to upset someone else. Please help me and my family.

Sincerely,

Yolanda, 15

Problem #4

I Hate School

I hate school. I hate it so much I skip school almost every day. Luckily, I am smart, and I'm in all the advanced classes so I don't have a reputation as a "bad kid." Only the people who really know me know about my strange feelings. My parents don't care. They don't even mention it if I don't go to school. What I end up doing is sleeping all day and then staying up all night talking to my friends. I get behind in my homework, but when I try to go back to school, all my teachers and friends get mad at me, so it makes me mad that I went back. I just get so depressed when I think about it. I am thinking about dropping out of school because I am 18 now, but I really don't want to do that because I realize it would ruin my life. I don't want to go back, but I also don't want it to ruin my life. I am so confused, and I have really tried to go back and just can't take it. What should I do? Please help.

Sincerely,

Luis, 18

Advice Columns Answer Sheet

Read through your teen problem with your group, and then answer the following questions in the space provided. Share your answers with the rest of the class.

What should the person (definitely) do?	What would happen if the person were to do that?	What else could the person (possibly) do?

Mix and Mingle Instructions

1. Each person has one question stem strip.

2. Find a partner.

3. Give a compliment to your partner.

4. Read the question on your strip.

5. Answer the question on your strip.

6. Listen to your partner compliment you.

7. Listen to your partner read his or her question.

8. Listen to your partner answer his or her question.

9. Find a new partner.

10. Do the same thing over again _____ times.

Reading Question Stem Chart

Word Meaning

Which words from paragraph ___ help the reader understand the meaning of the word?

In paragraph ___, the word ___ means ___.

Which of the following words is a synonym for the word ___?

Which of these is an antonym for the word ___?

Which words help the reader understand the meaning of the word ___?

Summary of Main Idea and Supporting Details

What is paragraph ___ mainly about?

What is this selection mainly about?

What is the primary purpose of paragraph ___?

Which statement best supports the idea that ___?

In paragraph ___, why does [character] say ___?

Why is the title of the story appropriate?

What is the best summary of paragraph(s) ___?

What is the best summary of the selection?

Conflict

When does the problem in the story begin?

What was the source of the author's conflict with [another character]?

What is the basic conflict in paragraph ___?

What does [character's] internal conflict stem from?

When does [character's] major conflict begin?

When does [character's] problem begin?

What is one conflict that [character] faces?

Theme

Which line best summarizes a theme of the story?

How is the theme in this story best revealed?

How is the theme best demonstrated?

Which sentence expresses a theme of the selection?

Plot Development

How does the author build suspense?

What does the author do at the climax of this story?

What surprising plot development occurs in paragraph ___?

How does the author develop the article?

Why did [character(s)] do ___?

Characterization

Which sentence from the story best conveys [character's] quality?

What do the actions of [character] in paragraph ___ disclose?

How is ___'s character best revealed?

What does [character's] response in paragraph ___ reveal?

In paragraph ___, why does [character] ___?

Which line from the story best reveals ___?

Setting

How does the [setting] affect [character's] ability to ___?

How does the [setting] affect the narrator's feelings toward [character]?

Which sentence from the article best helps the reader understand the author's feelings about the setting?

Point of View

What does the story's point of view allow the reader to understand?

Why is the first-person narration a good choice for this story?

Literary Forms

What is one way this story resembles a fable?

What does the author teach by using a parable?

In this story, what does ___ symbolize?

Which line from the story serves as an example of sarcasm?

Why does the author use repetition in paragraph ___?

Why does the author introduce the fact that ___?

How does the author primarily develop the selection?

continued

Reading Question Stem Chart (continued)

Conflict (continued)

Which of the following sentences from the article explains the author's primary conflict?

Inferential Thinking

What does the reader infer from paragraph ____?

What inference does paragraph ____ support?

What conclusion can be drawn from paragraph ____?

Which quotation from paragraph ____ best supports the generalization that ____?

In paragraph ____, what is the most likely reason [character] feels ____?

What kind of generalizations can be made about ____?

What may have been the author's reason for writing this selection?

What is the significance of ____?

From the tone in the first paragraph, what can the reader tell?

What is the primary purpose of the selection?

What tone does the author establish?

What is the tone of paragraph ____?

What can the reader conclude from the selection?

Characterization (continued)

What do [character's] actions as a boy/girl show?

What do [character's] thoughts indicate?

How does [character] change from the beginning of this selection to the end?

Figurative Language and Symbols

Which line uses metaphor to create a ____ effect?

For what is the ____ in paragraph ____ a metaphor?

When the author says ____, what is he/she suggesting?

Why does the author use the simile ____?

How does the author use figurative language to describe ____?

How does the author use sensory images to describe ____?

The ____ in paragraph ____ symbolizes ____.

What does ____ symbolize?

Why does [character] respond with figurative language in paragraph ____?

Why does the author use exclamation points in paragraph ____?

Why does the author use figurative language in paragraph ____?

Literary Forms (continued)

How does the author build suspense?

Why does the author use questions in paragraph ____?

Why does the author use a description in paragraph ____?

What does the author indicate by using the phrase ____?

Which quotation from the selection best summarizes the author's view?

Text Structure, Characteristics, and Historical Context

Which sentence from the selection explains the author's primary conflict?

Which audience would probably relate most to the selection's central message?

Why does the author change the time frame in paragraph ____?

What is the historical context that best contributes to the reader's understanding of paragraph ____?

In paragraph ____, what does the author want to emphasize by using the word ____?

Why does the author italicize words in the text, such as ____ and ____?

How does the author best develop this story?

What can the reader conclude about the author?

After reading the selection, what is a reasonable prediction?

What can the reader tell from the article?

How does the historical context affect [character]?

Reading Question Stem Cards

Main Idea and Supporting Details

- Paragraphs ___ and ___ are mostly about _____ .
- This selection is mainly about _____ .
- Paragraph ___ is mostly about _____ .
- Paragraphs ___ through ___ are mostly about _____ .
- The primary purpose of paragraph ___ is to _____ .
- Which statement best supports the idea that _____ ?
- In paragraph ___, [character] says _____ because _____ .
- The title of the story is appropriate because _____ .

Summaries

- Which of these is the best summary of paragraph(s) _____?
- Which of the following is the best summary of the selection?

Characterization

- Which sentence from the story best conveys [character's quality]?
- What do the actions of _____ in paragraph ____ disclose?
- _____'s character is best revealed through _____ .
- What does [character's] response in paragraph ___ reveal?
- In paragraph ___, the author describes [character] as "[doing something]" to show .
- Paragraph ___ reveals that _____ is _____ .
- In paragraph ____, [character] does _____ because _____ .
- Which line from the story best reveals _____ ?
- In trying to achieve his/her goal of _____, [character] could best be described as _____ .
- Paragraphs ___ through ___ show that the boy/girl [character] is _____ .
- In paragraphs ___ through ___, the [character's] thoughts indicate that he/she is .
- [Character] changes from the beginning of the selection to the end by _____ .
- By the end of the selection, [character] became _____ because of _____ .

Point of View

- The story's point of view allows the reader to understand that _____ .
- The first-person narration is a good choice for this story because _____ .

continued

Reading Question Stem Cards (continued)

Conflict

- The problem in the story begins when _____ .
- The source of the author's conflict with [another character] was _____ .
- What is the basic conflict in paragraph ____?
- [Character's] internal conflict stems from _____ .
- [Character's] major conflict begins when he/she _____ .
- [Character's] problem begins when _____ .
- What is one conflict that [character] faces?
- Which of the following sentences from the article explains the author's primary conflict?

Theme

- Which of the following lines best summarizes a theme of the story?
- The theme in this story is best revealed through _____ .
- The theme of _____ is best demonstrated through _____ .
- Which sentence expresses a theme of the selection?

Plot Development

- The author builds suspense by _____ .
- At the climax of this story, the author _____ .
- What surprising plot development occurs in paragraph ___?
- The author develops _____ when he/she _____ the selection by _____ .
- The author develops the selection by _____ .
- Why did [character(s)] do _____ ?

Setting

- How does the setting affect [character's] ability to _____ ?
- How does the setting affect the narrator's feelings toward [character]?
- Because this article is written about past events, the author _____ .
- Which sentence from the selection best helps the reader understand the author's feelings about the setting?

continued

Reading Question Stem Cards (continued)

Literary Forms

- One way this story resembles a fable is that _____ .

- This selection is best described as a _____. (Answer choices would be literary forms: tall tale, fable, and so on.)

- In paragraph ___, the author uses a parable to teach _____ .

- In this story, _____ symbolizes _____ .

- Which line from the story serves as an example of sarcasm?

- The author uses repetition in paragraph ___ to _____ .

- The author introduces the fact that _____ in order to _____
  _____ .

- The author develops the selection primarily through _____ .

- The author builds suspense by _____ .

- The author writes _____ to show _____ .

- The author uses questions in paragraph ___ to _____ .

- In paragraph ___, the author uses a description to _____ .

- The author includes a question at the end of paragraph ___ to show that _____ .

- The author uses the phrase _____ to indicate that _____ .

- Which quotation from the selection best summarizes the author's view that _____
  _____ ?

continued

Reading Question Stem Cards (continued)

Figurative Language and Symbols

- Which of the following lines uses metaphor to create a _____ effect?

- The _____ in paragraph ___ is a metaphor for _____ .

- When the author says _____ , he/she suggests that _____ .

- In paragraph ___, the author uses the simile "_____" to _____ .

- In paragraph ___, the author uses figurative language to describe _____ .

- In paragraph ___, the author uses sensory images to describe _____ .

- The _____ in paragraph ___ symbolizes _____ .

- What does _____ symbolize?

- Why does [character] respond with figurative language in paragraph _____?

- In paragraph _____, why does (or doesn't) the author show _____ finishing his/her sentence?

- Why does the author use exclamation points in paragraphs ___ through ___?

- In paragraph ___, why does (or doesn't) the author show _____?

- Why does the author respond with figurative language in paragraph ___?

Inferential Thinking

- Paragraph ___ allows the reader to infer that _____ .

- Paragraph ___ supports the inference that _____ .

- What conclusion can be drawn from paragraph ___?

- Which quotation from paragraph ___ best supports the generalization that _____ ?

- In paragraph ___, [character] most likely feels insulted because _____ .

- What kind of generalizations can be made about _____ ?

- What may have been the author's reason for writing this selection?

- By the end of the selection, [character] becomes a stronger person because of _____ .

- What is the significance of _____ ?

- From the tone in the first paragraph, the reader can tell that _____ .

- The reader can conclude that a primary purpose of the title of selection is to _____ .

- What tone does the author establish in paragraph ___?

- The tone of paragraph ___ is _____ .

- The reader can conclude _____ .

continued

Reading Question Stem Cards (continued)

Text Structures, Characteristics of the Text, and Historical Context

- Because the author describes the events of his/her life in the order in which they occurred, it is easier for the reader to _____ .

- Which of the following sentences from the selection explains the author's primary

- conflict?

- The audience that would probably relate most to the selection's central message would be _____ .

- The author changes the time frame in paragraphs ___ and ___ in order to _____ .

- The historical context that best contributes to the reader's understanding of paragraph ___ is _____ .

- In paragraph ___, the author uses the word _____ to emphasize _____ .

- Why does the author italicize words in the text, such as _____ and _____ ?

- The author best develops this story by _____ .

- The reader can conclude that the author _____ .

- It is reasonable to predict that _____ .

- The reader can tell from the article _____ .

- How does the [historical context] affect [character's] ability to _____ ?

Reading Question Stem Strips

Main Idea and Supporting Details

What is paragraph ___ mostly/mainly about?

Main Idea and Supporting Details

What is this selection mainly about?

Main Idea and Supporting Details

What is the primary purpose of paragraph ___?

Main Idea and Supporting Details

Which statement best supports the idea that ____ _____?

Main Idea and Supporting Details

In paragraph __, why does [character] say _____ _____ ?

Main Idea and Supporting Details

Why is the title of the selection appropriate?

Summaries

What is the best summary of paragraph(s) __?

Summaries

What is the best summary of the selection?

continued

Teaching Your Secondary ELLs the Language of Tests: Focusing on Language in English Language Arts
© 2009 r4 Educated Solutions • solution-tree.com • Visit go.solution-tree.com/ELL to download this page.

Reading Question Stem Strips (continued)

Theme

Which line best summarizes a theme of the story?

Theme

How is the theme in this story best revealed?

Theme

How is the theme best demonstrated?

Theme

Which sentence expresses a theme of the selection?

Setting

How does the setting affect [character's] ability to _____?

Setting

How does the setting affect the narrator's feelings toward [character]?

Setting

Which sentence from the article best helps the reader understand the author's feelings about the setting?

Characterization

Which sentence from the story best conveys [character's quality]?

continued

Reading Question Stem Strips (continued)

Characterization

What do the actions of [character] in paragraph ___ disclose?

Characterization

How is _____'s character best revealed?

Characterization

What does [character's] response in paragraph __ reveal?

Characterization

In paragraph __, why does [character] _____?

Characterization

Which line from the story best reveals _____?

Characterization

What do [character's] actions as a boy/girl show?

Characterization

What do [character's] thoughts indicate?

Characterization

How does [character] change from the beginning of the selection to the end?

continued

Reading Question Stem Strips (continued)

Point of View

What does the story's point of view allow the reader to understand?

Point of View

Why is the first-person narration a good choice for this story?

Conflict

When does the problem in the story begin?

Conflict

What was the source of the author's conflict with [another character]?

Conflict

What is the basic conflict in paragraph ____?

Conflict

When does [character's] major conflict begin?

Conflict

When does [character's] problem begin?

Conflict

What is one conflict that [character] faces?

continued

Reading Question Stem Strips (continued)

Conflict

Which of the following sentences from the selection explains the author's primary conflict?

Plot Development

How does the author build suspense?

Plot Development

What does the author do at the climax of this story?

Plot Development

What surprising plot development occurs in paragraph _____?

Plot Development

How does the author develop the selection?

Plot Development

Why did [character(s)] do _____?

Literary Forms

What is one way this story resembles a fable?

Literary Forms

What does the author teach by using a parable?

continued

Reading Question Stem Strips (continued)

Literary Forms

In this story, what does _____ symbolize?

Literary Forms

Which line from the story serves as an example of sarcasm?

Literary Forms

Why does the author use repetition in paragraph __?

Literary Forms

Why does the author introduce the fact that ____ _____?

Literary Forms

How does the author primarily develop the selection?

Literary Forms

How does the author build suspense?

Literary Forms

Why does the author use questions in paragraph __?

Literary Forms

Why does the author use a description in paragraph __?

---

continued

Reading Question Stem Strips (continued)

Literary Forms

What does the author indicate by using the phrase _____?

Literary Forms

Which quotation from the selection best summarizes the author's view?

Figurative Language and Symbols

Which line uses metaphor to create a _____ effect?

Figurative Language and Symbols

What is the _____ in paragraph __ a metaphor for?

Figurative Language and Symbols

When the author says _____, what is he/she suggesting?

Figurative Language and Symbols

Why does the author use the simile _____ ?

Figurative Language and Symbols

How does the author use figurative language to describe _____?

Figurative Language and Symbols

How does the author use sensory images to describe _____?

continued

Reading Question Stem Strips (continued)

Figurative Language and Symbols

The _____ in paragraph __ symbolizes _____.

Figurative Language and Symbols

What does _____ symbolize?

Figurative Language and Symbols

Why does [character] respond with figurative language in paragraph __?

Figurative Language and Symbols

Why does the author use exclamation points in paragraph __?

Figurative Language and Symbols

Why does the author use figurative language in paragraph __?

Inferential Thinking

What does the reader infer from paragraph __?

Inferential Thinking

What inference does paragraph __ support?

Inferential Thinking

What conclusion can be drawn from paragraph __?

continued

Reading Question Stem Strips (continued)

Inferential Thinking

Which quotation from paragraph __ best supports the generalization that _____?

Inferential Thinking

In paragraph __, what is the most likely reason [character] feels _____ ?

Inferential Thinking

What kind of generalizations can be made about _____?

Inferential Thinking

What may have been the author's reason for writing this selection?

Inferential Thinking

What is the significance of _____?

Inferential Thinking

From the tone in the first paragraph, what can the reader tell?

Inferential Thinking

What is the primary purpose of the selection?

Inferential Thinking

What tone does the author establish?

continued

Teaching Your Secondary ELLs the Language of Tests: Focusing on Language in English Language Arts
© 2009 r4 Educated Solutions • solution-tree.com • Visit **go.solution-tree.com/ELL** to download this page.

Reading Question Stem Strips (continued)

Inferential Thinking

What is the tone of paragraph __?

Inferential Thinking

What can the reader conclude from the selection?

Text Structures, Characteristics of the Text, and Historical Context

Which sentence from the selection explains the author's primary conflict?

Text Structures, Characteristics of the Text, and Historical Context

Which audience would probably relate most to the selection's central message?

Text Structures, Characteristics of the Text, and Historical Context

Why does the author change the time frame in paragraph __?

Text Structures, Characteristics of the Text, and Historical Context

What is the historical context that best contributes to the reader's understanding of paragraph __?

Text Structures, Characteristics of the Text, and Historical Context

In paragraph __, what does the author want to emphasize by using the word _____?

Text Structures, Characteristics of the Text, and Historical Context

Why does the author italicize words in the text, such as _____ and _____?

continued

Reading Question Stem Question Strips (continued)

Text Structures, Characteristics of the Text, and Historical Context

How does the author best develop this story?

Text Structures, Characteristics of the Text, and Historical Context

What can the reader conclude about the author?

Text Structures, Characteristics of the Text, and Historical Context

After reading the selection, what is a reasonable prediction?

Text Structures, Characteristics of the Text, and Historical Context

What can the reader tell from the article?

Text Structures, Characteristics of the Text, and Historical Context

How does the historical context affect [character]?

Chapter 2

Teaching the Language of Revising and Editing

Revising and Editing Through Warm-Ups

A *warm-up* is a short exercise that is completed by students before a lesson is delivered. Using warm-ups is a way of engaging students in learning as soon as they enter the classroom. When students are engaged in this way, they are more focused throughout the class period, and valuable instructional time is not lost.

Implications for High-Stakes Testing

Many English language arts and writing assessments include revising and editing sections that require students to make multiple changes to a selection. Doing short daily warm-ups that contain the types of errors found on these tests allows students to prepare for these portions of the assessment without long, tedious drill and practice.

Lesson Plan for Revising and Editing Through Warm-Ups

Materials

- Warm-Ups—Corrected (Days 1–5), for teacher use (page 74)

- Transparency of Warm-Ups—Uncorrected (Days 1–5) (page 78)

- Warm-Up Passages (Day 1), for teacher use (page 82)

- Proofreader's Marks handout, one per student (page 84)

- Red pencils or pens, one per student

- Glue, if using spiral notebooks

- Warm-up notebooks, one per student (either a spiral notebook or a pocket folder with brads containing notebook paper)

- Dry-erase markers, black and red

- Overhead marker, red

Academic Vocabulary

Understanding the meaning of the following terms is critical to a student's success in this lesson. It will not be possible—or practical—to teach all the words on this list at once, nor is this an exhaustive list of vocabulary that is necessary to know for this lesson. Also keep in mind that many students will already be familiar with many of these words.

brain	jog	proofreader
caret	muscles	revising
correction	participate	specific
editing	passage	stretch
error	procedure	warm-up
exercise		

Activities

1. Before implementing warm-ups as a daily bell-ringer activity, teach students what a warm-up is and what the classroom procedure will be.

2. Ask students if they know what a warm-up is. They may respond that it is something they do before class gets started, if they have experienced warm-ups in other classes. Ask them why it is called a warm-up.

3. Tell them that people usually perform a warm-up before participating in sports or exercising to literally warm up their muscles, so they will not get hurt. For example, before playing soccer, athletes might slowly jog or stretch to prepare their muscles and increase their heart rate. It is important that warm-ups be specific to the exercise that follows.

4. Similarly, the warm-ups that the students do in their English language arts class will be specific to the exercise, or the standardized test, that will follow. Just as the standardized test contains revising and editing portions, so will the students' warm-ups contain the same language of the test and the same types of errors to be found. By practicing warm-ups every day, the students will be well prepared for their test. The "muscle" that will be warmed up from these exercises is their brain.

5. Show the students a transparency of Warm-Ups—Uncorrected (Days 1–5). Cover the bottom four warm-ups with a piece of paper, so only the top sentence is visible. Move the paper down to show the second sentence and tell them that each day of the week, they will have a new sentence to correct for their warm-up. Explain that the warm-ups come from a passage that will be read to them.

6. Hand out a Warm-Up Notebook (see figure 2.1) to each student, and hold one up to show students how to use it. On the cover, show them where to write *Warm-Ups* and where to put their name and class period. On the first page, tell students to write the date and to copy the first sentence from the transparency, exactly as it is written.

7. Hand out red pencils or pens, or ask students to get out their red pencils or pens. Tell the students that the sentence has errors in it that they will correct in red using proofreader's marks. Hand out a copy of Proofreader's Marks to each student, and have them glue the paper onto the inside cover of their warm-up notebooks (to fit inside some spiral notebooks, the handout may need to be trimmed). Review the most commonly used editing marks, such as the caret, and tell the students that they will learn the marks through practice.

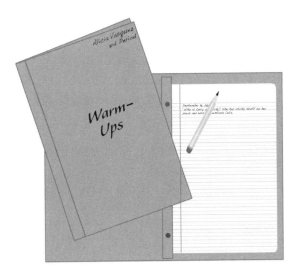

Figure 2.1: This is an example of a warm-up notebook.

8. Read the Warm-Up Passage (Day 1) aloud to the class, but do not give the students a copy of it because it is written correctly. Model for the students how to complete the first warm-up by copying the first set of sentences from the Warm-Ups—Uncorrected (Days 1–5) transparency on the board in black marker. A corrected version of the Warm-Ups (Days 1–5) is on page 74.

Why is Lucy all sticky. she has sticky stuff on her pause and ears? questions Celia.

9. Read the sentence aloud. Ask students these questions (using the language of standardized testing): **What change, if any, should be made in sentence 1?** (editing errors) **What revision, if any, is needed in sentence 1?** (revising errors)

10. Allow the students to respond and make corrections as needed on the first set of sentences on the board with a red dry-erase marker, using proofreader's marks and pointing out to students where the marks can be found on their handout. (Learning the marks may or may not be required by the teacher, but the students will become familiar with them with practice.) Ask the students to copy the corrections in their sentences in their warm-up notebooks.

11. Tell the students that when they do a warm-up the next time, they will be able to come up to the overhead and make corrections on the transparency.

12. Have students copy the next sentence on the Warm-Ups—Uncorrected (Days 1–5) into their notebooks. Ask the revising and editing questions, and then ask for volunteers to come up to the overhead to make the corrections on the transparency. When the sentence is corrected, tell the students to copy the corrections into their notebooks.

13. Have students close their notebooks. Collect them and place them in a bin or box that is accessible to the students. Collect the red pencils or pens, and place them in a container near the notebooks. Tell students that at the beginning of each class period they are to get their warm-up notebook and a red pencil or pen, go to their desks, write the date on the first available line in black pen or pencil, proceed to copy the warm-up from the transparency into their notebooks, and make their corrections with a red pencil or pen. When all students have finished, the teacher will discuss the changes the students made to the warm-up, and volunteers will make the changes on the transparency with the red overhead marker.

14. In the days following, before each class period begins, have the warm-up transparency placed on the overhead with the appropriate warm-up uncovered. It may or may not be necessary to reread the passage every day. Allow only 5 to 10 minutes for the warm-up activity.

Suggestions

- Set a timer for the same amount of time each day to create a daily routine.

- Choose two students who are always early to class to distribute the Warm-Up Notebooks and red pencils or pens to the other students.

Revising and Editing Question Stems and Responses During Warm-Ups

Questioning is an instructional approach that enables students to internalize academic language as they use it in discussions with their teacher and other students. The goal is for all students to interact in class through the structured support of revising and editing question stems and responses. It is important to provide multiple opportunities for interaction and discussion. This supplies the much-needed oral rehearsal necessary for both English language acquisition and content development (Echevarria, Short, & Vogt, 2004).

Implications for High-Stakes Testing

By using the question stems and response sentence frames found in the revising and editing portions of standardized assessments, teachers can support oral language interaction activities for students while familiarizing them with the academic language of the test. As students practice questioning and responding to their teacher and to each other, they integrate the written academic language of the test into extended academic talk. Then, when they come in contact with this language on a standardized test, students will easily recognize and understand it. This familiarity promotes confidence.

Lesson Plan for Reading and Editing Question Stems and Responses During Warm-Ups

Materials

- Transparencies of Warm-Ups—Uncorrected (Days 1–5), (page 78)

- Revising and Editing Question Stems handout, one per student (page 85)

- Revising and Editing Responses handout, one per student (page 86)

- Revising and Editing Academic Vocabulary Cards, printed on cardstock and cut out, one teacher set (pages 87–88)

- Students' Warm-Up Notebooks

Academic Vocabulary

Understanding the meaning of the following terms is critical to a student's success in this lesson. It will not be possible—or practical—to teach all the words on this list at once, nor is this an exhaustive list of vocabulary that is necessary to know for this lesson. Also keep in mind that many students will already be familiar with many of these words.

beginning	following	phrase
change	improve	revision
clarified	insert	rewrite
combine	logically	sentence
delete	move	support
effective	organization	switch
end	paragraph	transition

Activities

This lesson can be used in conjunction with the Revising and Editing Through Warm-Ups lesson beginning on page 67.

1. Before putting the Revising and Editing Question Stems and Responses into practice in the classroom, teach students the procedures for completing warm-ups.

2. Give each student copies of the Revising and Editing Question Stems and Revising and Editing Responses handouts, which can be placed inside the Warm-Up Notebooks. If desired, large posters of the question stems and responses can be made and placed in an easily visible part of the room.

3. Explicitly teach the academic vocabulary in the question stems and responses by having the students pantomime the meaning of the word meanings using the Revising and Editing Academic Vocabulary Cards. For example, a student representing the word *beginning* might place several other students in a line and then stand at the front of the line holding the vocabulary card *beginning*. A student pantomiming the meaning of the word *switch* might place three students in a row and then exchange places with one of the students or exchange vocabulary cards with another student.

4. Read through the questions and the responses with the students, pointing out the academic vocabulary words. Explain that the wording is exactly the same as the wording on the revising and editing portion of the standardized test they will be taking.

5. Explain to students that when they are correcting warm-ups or discussing revisions to be made to any piece of writing, they will be expected to use the revising and editing question stems and responses on the handouts in their warm-up notebooks.

6. Model the use of the stems by reviewing a warm-up the students have completed, so they are already familiar with the edits. Correct the errors by asking and answering with the stems from the handouts. Place a warm-up on the overhead and ask, **What change, if any, should be made in this sentence?** Point out that the sentence is on the Revising and Editing Question Stems handout and will be seen on standardized tests. If the students answer, "Add a comma between *him* and *then*," reply: **Which response could you use from the Revising and Editing Responses handout that means the same thing?** Help the students find the response: "Insert a comma after *him*." Explain that the response means the same thing as the question stem. Continue to encourage students to substitute the responses from the handout for their own language and explain to them that they are "speaking" the academic language of the test.

7. After the question stems and responses have been introduced and modeled, insist that students use them when interacting about correcting warm-ups in class.

Suggestions

- Allow students to work on warm-ups in pairs at times, so they can practice both the questions and the responses.

- Allow students to take turns being the teacher and asking all the questions.

Warm-Ups—Corrected (Days 1–5)

The Mystery of the Cinnamon Rolls

Day 1

"Why is Lucy all sticky? She has sticky stuff on her paws and ears?" questions Celia.

"I'm sure it's something from outside," replies Sofia.

Day 2

"Hey! Look!" shouts Roberto, holding an empty cinnamon roll carton.

"What happened to my cinnamon rolls? I'd only eaten one so far," says Sofia.

Day 3

Celia ponders the clues for a moment. Then she reaches over and sniffs Lucy's ears.

Day 4

Lucy smells like cinnamon. "I think I know what happened to your cinnamon rolls," Celia grins.

Making Tamales

Day 5

"Yummy! Tamales are delicious," says Roberto.

"I'm going to make some tamales on Thanksgiving. Do you want to come help me?" asks Celia's mom.

Warm-Ups—Corrected (Days 6–10)

Making Tamales (cont.)

Day 6

"I'd love to. Ooh! I'm going to make some tamales!" smiles Roberto.

"You don't know what you're getting yourself into. When my uncle helped once and only once, he learned it was too much work." He prefers to buy them rather than make them," advises Celia.

Day 7

The next day, Roberto is anxious to get started. As Celia's mom prepares the meat, Celia, Roberto, and Sofia begin spreading the masa (dough) on the corn husks. After a couple dozen, Roberto gets restless.

Day 8

"This really is hard work," complains Roberto. He doesn't realize he has masa everywhere, including in his hair. Minutes later, Roberto asks, "Are we finished yet?"

Day 9

Finally, Celia's mom announces, "Tamales are ready!" Roberto rushes over to devour his hard work. As he takes a bite, Roberto whispers to Celia, "Next time your mom wants me to help make tamales, tell her I'm busy."

Allison

Day 10

Allison she changed my life. No she wasn't my girlfriend. In June 2001, when Tropical Storm Allison hit.

Warm-Ups—Corrected (Days 11–15)

Allison (cont.)

Day 11

My mom had gone to a concert in San Antonio with her sisters. I stayed home to take care of my little sister. We were sitting on the couch watching TV that night when it started raining.

Day 12

I rolled my eyes, thinking, "Great, now the yard is going to be muddy, and my baby sister won't not be able to play outside tomorrow. I guess I'll have to think of something else to do." It kept raining.

Day 13

And it kept raining. I noticed the water started seeping in from under the door. I put down some towels to soak it up, but it kept raining.

Day 14

By midnight, water was creeping into the house. and I couldn't sleep, and I didn't know what to do, and Around five in the morning, the water inside the house was up to my knees. And it kept raining.

Day 15

I tried to call for help, but not one of the phone lines worked. By late morning, the water was up to my waist, and it kept rising.

Warm-Ups—Corrected (Days 16–20)

Allison (cont.)

Day 16

I grabbed my four-year-old sister and swam out of the house to a nearby office building. I climbed into the attic, hoping we would be safe. It kept raining.

Day 17

It finally stopped. I looked at us. We were a mess. The filthy flood waters had saturated our clothes and hair. We didn't smell no good, either.

Day 18

Hours later as I sat thinking about what to do next, I heard a familiar voice shouting my name. I peered outside.

Day 19

It was my cousin with a stranger in a boat. They'd come to rescue us. I waved and yelled to her from the window.

Day 20

I carried my little sister out, and the man with my cousin helped us into the boat. As we moved farther and farther away, one tear rolled down my cheek.

Warm-Ups—Uncorrected (Days 1–5)

The Mystery of the Cinnamon Rolls

Day 1

Why is Lucy all sticky. she has sticky stuff on her pause and ears? questions Celia.

Im sure its some thing from out side, replies Sofia.

Day 2

hey! Look! shouted Roberto holding an empty cinnamon role carton.

What happen to my cinnamon roles? Id only ate one so far Says Sofia.

Day 3

Celia ponder the clues for a moment. Then reaches over and sniffs Lucys' ears.

Day 4

Lucy smell like cinnamon. "I think I know what happen to you cinnamon rolls." Celia grins.

Making Tamales

Day 5

Yummy…tamales are delishus says Roberto.

Im going to make some on thanksgiving do you want to come help me. asked Celia mom.

Warm-Ups—Uncorrected (Days 6–10)

Making Tamales (cont.)

Day 6

I'd love to. Ooh Im going to make me some tamales! smiles Roberto.

"You don't no what your getting yourself into. When my uncle helped once and only once he learned it was to much work." He prefer to bye them then make them advises Celia

Day 7

The next day roberto is anxshus to get started. As Celias mom prepare the meat Celia Roberto and Sofia begin spreading the masa (dough) on the corn husks After a couple dozen Roberto got restless.

Day 8

This realy is hard work complains Roberto He doesnt realize he has masa everywhere including in his hair Minutes later Roberto asks Are we finished yet

Day 9

Finally Celias mom announce tamales are ready. Roberto rushes over too devour his hard work. As he take a bite Roberto wisper to Celia Next time your mom wants me to help make tamales tell her Im busy

Allison

Day 10

Allison she changed my life. No she weren't my girlfriend. In june 2001 when Tropical Storm Allison hit.

Warm-Ups—Uncorrected (Days 11–15)

Allison (cont.)

Day 11

My mom had went to a consert in san antonio with her sisters' I staid home to take care of my little sister. We were sitting on the couch watching tv that night it started raining.

Day 12

I rolled my eyes thinking great now the yard is gonna be muddy and my baby sister won't not be able to play outside tomorrow I guess I have to think of some thing else to do, it kept raining.

Day 13

And it kept raining. I noticed the water start seeping in from under the door. I put down some towel to soak it up but it keep raining.

Day 14

By midnight water was creeping into the house and I couldn't sleep and I didn't know what to do and around five in the morning, the water inside the house is up to my knees. And it kept raining.

Day 15

I tried to call for help, but not one of the phone lines worked. By late morning, the water was up to my waist, and it kept rising.

Warm-Ups—Uncorrected (Days 16–20)

Allison (cont.)

Day 16

I grabbed my four year old sister and swum out of the house to a near by office building I climbed into the attic hopping we would be safe. It kept raining.

Day 17

It finally stopped. I looked at we. We were a messy. The filthy flood waters had saturated our close and hair We didnt smell no good either.

Day 18

Hours later as I sit thinking about what to due next I hear a familiar voice shouting my name. I peered outside.

Day 19

It was my cousin wit a stranger in a boat. Theyd came to rescue us. I waved and yelled to she from the window.

Day 20

I carried my little sister out and the man with me cousin hept us into the boat. As we moved farther and farther away one tear rolled down my cheek.

Warm-Up Passages

The warm-ups are for teacher use only, and are written as stories. On the first day, read the entire passage all the way through. Then do revisions of each portion one day at a time as a daily warm-up at the beginning of class. Use the language of the Revising and Editing Question Stems and Responses to correct the warm-ups together in class.

Passage 1 (Days 1–4)
The Mystery of the Cinnamon Rolls

"Why is Lucy all sticky? She has sticky stuff on her paws and ears," questions Celia.

"I'm sure it's something from outside," replies Sofia.

"Hey! Look!" shouts Roberto, holding an empty cinnamon roll carton.

"What happened to my cinnamon rolls? I'd only eaten one so far," says Sofia.

Celia ponders the clues for a moment. Then she reaches over and sniffs Lucy's ears.

Lucy smells like cinnamon. "I think I know what happened to your cinnamon rolls," Celia grins.

Passage 2 (Days 5–9)
Making Tamales

"Yummy! Tamales are delicious," says Roberto.

"I'm going to make some tamales on Thanksgiving. Do you want to come help me?" asks Celia's mom.

"I'd love to. Ooh! I'm going to make some tamales!" smiles Roberto.

"You don't know what you're getting yourself into. When my uncle helped once and only once, he learned it was too much work. He prefers to buy them rather than make them," advises Celia.

The next day Roberto is anxious to get started. As Celia's mom prepares the meat, Celia, Roberto, and Sofia begin spreading the masa (dough) on the corn husks. After a couple dozen, Roberto gets restless.

"This really is hard work," complains Roberto. He doesn't realize he has masa everywhere, including in his hair. Minutes later, Roberto asks, "Are we finished yet?"

Finally, Celia's mom announces, "Tamales are ready!" Roberto rushes over to devour his hard work. As he takes a bite, Roberto whispers to Celia, "Next time your mom wants me to help make tamales, tell her I'm busy."

Warm-Up Passages (continued)

Passage 3 (Days 10–20)
Allison

Allison changed my life. No, she wasn't my girlfriend. In June 2001, Tropical Storm Allison hit.

My mom had gone to a concert in San Antonio with her sisters. I stayed home to take care of my little sister. We were sitting on the couch watching TV that night when it started raining.

I rolled my eyes, thinking, "Great, now the yard is going to be muddy, and my baby sister won't be able to play outside tomorrow. I guess I'll have to think of something else to do." It kept raining.

And it kept raining. I noticed the water started seeping under the door. I put down some towels to soak it up, but it kept raining.

By midnight, water was creeping into the house. I couldn't sleep, and I didn't know what to do. Around five in the morning, the water inside the house was up to my knees. And it kept raining.

I tried to call for help, but not one of the phone lines worked. By late morning, the water was up to my waist, and it kept rising.

I grabbed my four-year-old sister and swam out of the house to a nearby office building. I climbed into the attic hoping we would be safe. It kept raining.

It finally stopped. I looked at us. We were a mess. The filthy flood waters had saturated our clothes and hair. We didn't smell good, either.

Hours later as I sat thinking about what to do next, I heard a familiar voice shouting my name. I peered outside.

It was my cousin with a stranger in a boat. They'd come to rescue us. I waved and yelled to her from the window.

I carried my little sister out, and the man with my cousin helped us into the boat. As we moved farther and farther away, one tear rolled down my cheek.

Proofreader's Marks

Mark	Meaning	Example
ℓ	Delete	Our ~~our~~ reunion
◡	Close up, no space	My grand mother
ℰ	Delete and close up	My grand father
#	Insert space	family room
∧	Insert word or letter	fam͜ly
∼	Transpose	sist͜re
⩘	Insert comma	make a list inviting
⊙	Insert period	Hope for the best
⩒	Insert apostrophe	your sisters cousin
⊙	Insert colon	Invite the following
⩘	Insert semicolon	planned a picnic however
=	Insert hyphen	sister in law
⩗	Insert quotation marks	a fancy dinner
stet...	Restore to original	wanted to play ~~many~~ games (stet)
¶ / No ¶	Start new paragraph (or no paragraph intended if preceded by a "no")	We made our lists ¶ First No ¶ We made our lists. First
≡	Capitalize	aunt Carol
/	Lowercase	my Uncle
( )	Parentheses	the surprise guest John and Jane came
[ ]	Brackets	"to the [perfect] camp"
⬯	Spell out	He came Sat. evening
‖	Align	• Make a list • Find a place • Assign jobs
[	Move left	Make a list
]	Move right	Make a list
∨	Superscript	4th
∧	Subscript	H2O

Revising and Editing Question Stems

What change, if any, should be made in sentence _____?

What transition could/should be added to the beginning of sentence _____
_____?

Which transition [word or phrase] could best be added to the beginning of sentence _____?

What revision, if any, is needed in sentence _____?

What is the most effective way to revise/rewrite sentence _____?

What is the most effective way to improve the organization of the _____ paragraph?

What is the most effective way to rewrite the ideas in sentence _____?

What is the most effective way to combine sentences _____ and _____?

Which of these ideas could most logically be added after sentence _____?

The meaning of sentence _____ can be clarified by changing _____ to _____?

How should sentences _____ and _____ be rewritten?

_____ wants to add [this/the following] sentence to the _____ paragraph. Where is the best place to insert this sentence?

Which sentence could follow and support sentence _____?

Which sentence could best follow sentence _____ to support the idea in that sentence?

Make no change.

Revising and Editing Responses

Delete _____.

Delete the _____ after _____.

Change _____ to _____.

Insert _____ after _____.

Delete sentence _____.

Switch sentences _____ and _____.

Move sentence _____ to the beginning of the paragraph.

Move sentence _____ to the end of the paragraph.

Move sentence _____ so that it follows sentence _____.

Make no change.

No revision is needed.

Revising and Editing Academic Vocabulary Cards

beginning	end
change	following
clarified	improve
combine	insert
delete	logically
effective	move

continued

Revising and Editing Academic Vocabulary Cards
(continued)

organization	sentence
paragraph	support
phrase	switch
revision	transition
rewrite	

Chapter 3

Teaching the Language of the Open-Ended Response

Plot Elements

This sample lesson illustrates how a teacher can teach explicitly the components of the literary elements using graphic organizers. The topic chosen for instruction is plot elements. Students need to be taught each literary element individually. As each element is taught, students can add it to their Plot Elements chart (page 100) to keep a record of their learning.

Implications for High-Stakes Testing

A knowledge of literary elements is key to understanding the language of both the multiple-choice questions and the open-ended or short-answer response questions on the English language arts and reading portions of standardized assessments. On these tests, students are required to analyze fiction for literary elements.

Lesson Plan for Plot Elements

Materials

- Plot Elements handout (page 100), one per student and one transparency

- Plot Elements Sort Cards (page 101), one set per pair of students, cut out

- Plot Elements Mountain handout (page 102), unlabeled, one copy and one transparency

- Plot Terms Cards (page 103, either copied onto paper or written on sticky notes), one set, cut out

- Story Section Cards (page 104, either copied onto paper or written on sticky notes), one set, cut out

- Individual copies of literary text containing selections previously read by students

---

Academic Vocabulary

Understanding the meaning of the following terms is critical to a student's success in this lesson. It will not be possible—or practical—to teach all the words on this list at once, nor is this an exhaustive list of vocabulary that is necessary to know for this lesson. Also keep in mind that many students will already be familiar with many of these words.

antagonist	falling action	resolution
character	hero	rising action
climax	ingredients	section
conflict	intense	setting
element	internal	term
exposition	plot	villain
external	protagonist	

Activities

The Plot Elements Mountain handout has blanks for cards that are the size of a 3 x 3–inch sticky note. If desired, they can be used instead of cutting out the cards on the handout.

1. Group students into pairs and give each pair a set of Plot Elements Sort Cards. Tell the students that by guessing, they are to match the terms with their definitions. When they are finished, tell students that today they are going to learn the meanings of all the terms on their sort cards.

2. Ask students what good movies they have seen lately. After entertaining multiple answers, discuss what made them good movies. Seek various responses such as the actors, the movie's action, and its special effects. Ask the students what bad movies they have seen and why those movies were bad.

3. Explain to students that the same things that make a good movie are the elements that make good literature, but with different names. For example, in movies there are *actors,* but in literature there are *characters.* In movies, there is *action,* but in literature the action is called *plot.* Some movies may be bad or boring because they have no plot.

4. Tell students that this lesson will focus on the literary element of plot. Place a paper copy of the Plot Elements Mountain handout on the board at the front of the classroom and the transparency on the overhead.

5. Explain that plot is the literary element that describes the structure or organization of a story and that the structure looks like a mountain.

6. Show the class that the story begins at the bottom of the Plot Elements Mountain handout by pointing to the bottom left of the mountain. Explain that the beginning of the story is called the *exposition.* Tell students the exposition introduces the characters (the people in the story) and setting (the time and place of the story). Help students remember the word *exposition* by comparing it to the word *explain,* and tell them that the exposition explains who is in the story and when and where it happens. Write *Exposition Explains* on the board to the side of the graphic, and pantomime "explaining" by opening and closing hands like puppets talking, while saying the words.

7. Point to the left side of the Plot Elements Mountain handout on the graphic, and tell the students that this represents the plot's "rising action." The rising action is the series of conflicts and events that happen in the story. Discuss conflict and how it can either be internal (such as Goldilocks' conflict with herself when she was deciding whether to enter the three bears' house) or external (such as the conflict between Goldilocks and the bears when she was discovered).

Help students remember the term *rising action* by reminding them that the rising sun begins the day and shines its light on the day's events, just as the rising action does at the start of the story. Write *Rising Action* on the board to the side of the graphic near the Plot Elements Mountain handout, draw a rising sun (see figure 3.1 for an example) next to the words, and pantomime a sun rising while saying the words.

Figure 3.1: The Rising Action graphic could look like this.

8. Point to the top of the mountain and tell the students that the highest point on the mountain signifies what is called the *climax* of the story. This is the most intense, exciting point, and when it happens, the reader knows how the story will end. Discuss examples of different climaxes in movies students have seen. Help them remember the term *climax* by telling them that the story "climbs to the climax" just like a mountain climber climbs up a mountain. The climax comes when the climber reaches the top of the mountain and plants the flag. Write *Climb to the Climax* on the board above the graphic by the top of the Plot Elements Mountain handout, draw a stick figure planting a flag on the peak of the mountain (see figure 3.2), and pantomime proudly planting a flag while saying the words.

Figure 3.2: This is an example of how the Climb to the Climax graphic could look.

9. Point to the right side of the mountain below the peak and tell the students that this represents the "falling action" of the story. The falling action consists of the events and action that follow the climax when the characters solve the problems that caused the conflict, leading to the story's end. Discuss the falling action that occurred in the movies discussed previously. The movie did not just immediately end after the climax. Help students remember the term *falling action* by telling them that the mountain climber who climbed to the top of the mountain, or the climax, is now descending, or falling. Write *Falling Action* on the board next to the graphic by the right side of the Plot Elements Mountain handout, draw a stick figure falling off the mountain, and pantomime falling while saying the words (see figure 3.3).

Figure 3.3: The Falling Action graphic could look like this.

10. Point to the bottom-right side of the mountain and tell the students that this represents the "resolution" of the story, which comes at the conclusion, or end, of the story. Discuss the resolutions that occur in the previously discussed movies. Some were happy, some were sad, and some left the viewer with unanswered questions. Help students remember the term *resolution* by telling them that a resolution usually ends things, and people always remember the resolution. Tell them to "remember the resolution!" Write "Remember the Resolution!" on the board next to the graphic by the right side of the Plot Elements Mountain handout and pantomime a patriotic gesture, such as raising an arm in the air and pointing upward while saying the words.

11. Review the parts of the Plot Elements Mountain handout by repeating the mnemonic devices several times until students feel comfortable with them.

- Exposition (pantomime puppet hands talking)

- Rising Action (pantomime a rising sun)

- Climb to the Climax (pantomime climbing and planting a flag at the top of a mountain)

- Falling Action (pantomime falling off the mountain)

- Remember the Resolution (raise an arm in the air, pointing upward)

12. Erase the plot element terms on the board around the Plot Elements Mountain handout, and select five students to come to the front. Give each of them one of the Plot Terms Cards, and ask them to place them on the handout in the proper places. Once they have placed their cards, ask students to read their cards aloud. Discuss with the class whether the cards are placed correctly. After all cards are correctly placed, thank the participants and remove the cards.

13. Select five different students to come to the front of the classroom, and give each of them one of the Story Section Cards. Ask them to create a Plot Mountain with their cards by holding the cards in front of them in the correct corresponding position on the mountain. When they have decided on their card's position, ask each to read their Story Section Card. Again discuss with the class whether the cards are in the correct places. Then have the five students place their Story Section Cards on the Plot Elements Mountain handout in the proper place.

14. Tell students to return to their partners from the beginning of the lesson and ask them to match the Plot Elements Sort Cards terms with their definitions again. This time the pairs should easily be able to determine the terms' meanings by checking the Plot Elements Mountain handout at the front of the room. When the students are finished, check for accuracy as a class and have all students copy the definitions into their notes.

15. In subsequent lessons, give each student a copy of the Plot Elements handout. Explain that they are to complete the handout for each literary selection they read. Model the use of the graphic organizer by using the transparency. Fill in the name of the selection and discuss the characters and the setting before writing them down. The graphic organizer may be completed individually, in pairs, or in small groups. When students have finished, discuss their choices.

Characterization

This sample lesson illustrates how a teacher can teach explicitly the components of literary elements. The topic chosen for instruction is characterization and the five elements authors address in creating characters: appearance, actions, thoughts, speech, and reactions of others. Using fairy tales is a good way to introduce new concepts to English language learners of all ages because most cultures are familiar with some version of the basic tales.

Implications for High-Stakes Testing

Characterization is an inferential skill that students need to develop for the literary analysis that will be required on standardized tests. Usually, both multiple-choice objective reading sections and open-ended response sections require students to analyze characters.

Lesson Plan for Characterization

Materials

- Stick Figure Characterization handout (page 105), several copies per student and one transparency

- Characterization Chart handout (page 106), one transparency, one copied onto chart paper, and one copy per student

- Character Traits handout (pages 107–108), one per student

- Fairy tale of choice, preferably a picture book

- Large plain stick figure, drawn on chart paper or one transparency

Academic Vocabulary

Understanding the meaning of the following terms is critical to a student's success in this lesson. It will not be possible—or practical—to teach all the words on this list at once, nor is this an exhaustive list of vocabulary that is necessary to know for this lesson. Also keep in mind that many students will already be familiar with many of these words.

anonymously	graphic organizer	reaction
appropriate	guess	response
appearance	inappropriate	speech
author	infer	stick figure
character	looks	story
characterization	personal	thoughts
fairy tale	private	

Activities

1. Prior to class, draw a plain stick figure on one piece of chart paper and copy the Characterization Chart onto another piece (see figure 3.4). Place them on the wall at the front of the room. If preferred, use transparencies one at a time, but their size will limit the amount of information that can be written on them.

Figure 3.4: This is an example of the stick figure and Characterization Chart.

2.   Ask students when they meet someone new, how they know what kind of person he or she is. Prompt students until you have these answers:

   • Speech, or what they say (Draw a large speech bubble by the stick figure's head.)

   • Actions, or what they do (Draw a large rectangle around the stick figure's feet.)

   • Thoughts, or what they are thinking (Draw a large thought bubble by the stick figure's head.)

   • Appearance, or how they look (Draw a mirror in the stick figure's hand and a box next to the mirror.)

   • Reactions of others, or what others say or think (Draw a thought bubble and a speech bubble coming from the side of the paper.)

3.   Write the elements' names in the appropriate areas on the Stick Figure graphic.

4.   Discuss examples of information students have learned about others through these five elements. Ask questions about what they can tell about someone by observing these things, such as the following: **What might you know about a person who wears wrinkled clothes? What does it tell you if a person has lots of friends? What can you tell about a person who yells a lot? What can you tell about a person who speaks softly and always looks down? What could you tell about someone who always remembers your birthday? What can you tell about someone who cheats on a test? What can you tell about someone who cries when they hear a sad story?**

5.   Discuss with students that when they observe others in these ways and make conclusions about them, they are making educated guesses about these students. This is called *inferring*. Write the word on the board, and explain that students must become very good at inferring in order to understand literature. Explain to them that many times, the answer to a question about a character will not be written in the text, but they will be able to find the answer by looking at the character's speech, actions, thoughts, appearance, and/or at the reactions of others to the character.

6.   Explain that authors create characters using these five elements (speech, action, thoughts, appearance, and/or the reactions of others) and that readers get to know characters the same way that the students get to know each other. Point to each of the five areas on the Characterization Chart, and have students repeat the headings several times until they are comfortable with pronunciations.

7. Pass out copies of the Stick Figure Characterization handout. Explain to students that they will fill out the graphic organizer with information about a classmate or someone else at school known to everyone in the class. The descriptions should be anonymous. Instruct the students not to include the person's name. At this point, it may be a good idea to discuss what is and is not appropriate to write about in the classroom setting. For example, students may have heard a coach use some colorful language on the field or during a game, but it would not be appropriate to write that language on the handout. Instead, the students could write something more general, such as "uses bad words when mad at ref" or "sometimes swears when we lose." It would also be inappropriate to report private or personal details about a fellow student or ones that have been told in confidence. It is advisable to discuss several appropriate and inappropriate examples before beginning this activity. When everyone is finished, collect all the completed handouts, choose a few to read to the class, and have students guess who each characterization is about.

8. After the students have completed the handouts, the teacher has read several of them aloud, and the guessing activity is finished, discuss what made some of the Stick Figure Characterization handout entries interesting.

9. Give each student another copy of the Stick Figure Characterization handout. Place a transparency of the handout on the overhead. Tell students that they will be filling in the handout about the main character in a fairy tale that you will read to them.

10. Read a picture book of a fairy tale aloud, showing students the illustrations. Stop frequently to discuss the elements of characterization—speech, actions, thoughts, appearance, and reactions of others—as they occur in the story. Allow students to come to the overhead and fill in the Stick Figure Characterization handout each time one of the five elements is depicted in the story. Tell students to transfer what is written on the transparency to their handouts.

11. After reading the story, discuss the students' completed handouts, and explain that now they will fill out another handout about a different character in the story. Place the students in small groups or pairs, and allow them to choose a character. Give each pair or group another copy of the Stick Figure Characterization handout, have them work together to complete it, and then share their responses with the class.

12. Give each pair or group another copy of the Stick Figure Characterization handout and one of the Characterization Chart handout. Place the Characterization Chart handout transparency on the overhead, and model how to transfer the information from the Stick Figure Characterization to the chart using a student example of a completed Stick Figure Characterization handout. Explain that after completing the Stick Figure Characterization handout for the character of their choice, students will complete the chart for the fairy tale, adding that character to the chart.

13. In subsequent lessons, use both of the characterization graphic organizers with selections the students read in class.

Suggestions

- Have students add textual evidence to the Characterization Chart handout with quotes from the selection that support their responses.

- Another option is for students to include the page numbers where the textual evidence can be found.

- Discuss with students what character traits are and how they can be identified through the five elements that portray the character. Give each student a copy of the Character Traits handout, and have them choose several traits to describe their character and add them to their chart.

Open-Ended Test Question Stems

Asking open-ended questions is an essential component of good instruction. Open-ended questions encourage discussion and create opportunities for students to verbalize their understanding, thoughts, and ideas. This also allows English language learners to hear academic language as they listen to the responses of others. All open-ended questions and discussions should demand relevant, accurate, and specific textual evidence.

Implications for High-Stakes Testing

Open-ended responses on the reading portions of many standardized tests require a higher level of exploration and critical thinking than a one-word or one-sentence response. Students need to learn that their answers to open-ended questions not only require a reasonable idea, but must also be supported with appropriate textual evidence. It is necessary for students to practice this skill through class discussions to build accuracy, precision, and depth in their responses.

Lesson Plan for Open-Ended Test Question Stems

Materials

- Open-Ended Response Questions handout (pages 109–114), one per student and one transparency

- Chart paper, one sheet per group

- English language arts (ELA) textbooks, one per student

Academic Vocabulary

Understanding the meaning of the following terms is critical to a student's success in this lesson. It will not be possible—or practical—to teach all the words on this list at once, nor is this an exhaustive list of vocabulary that is necessary to know for this lesson. Keep in mind that many students will already be familiar with many of these words.

article	literary	respondent
closed	nonfiction	response
crossover	open-ended	selection
evidence	proof	stem (noun)
expository	prove	support
fiction	reflect	

Activities

1. Ask students what the difference is between an open-ended question and a closed question. Explain that a closed question has one right answer and it is usually short. Examples of closed questions are the following:

    - **How old is the narrator?**

    - **What is the setting of the story?**

    Explain that the answer to an open-ended question could have many correct responses, is longer, and requires more time to answer because the respondent must think, reflect, and then support the answer with evidence, or proof. Examples of open-ended questions are as follows:

    - **How do the narrator's actions reveal her feelings for her father?**

    - **What impact does the setting have on the story?**

2. Discuss the open-ended response questions that are often found on the English language arts portion of the standardized test that students will take. Place the transparency of the Open-Ended Response Questions handout on the overhead, and distribute a copy of the handout to each student. Explain that these are examples of the questions that appear on many standardized tests. Tell students that there are three types of questions: literary, expository, and a crossover of literary and expository. The *literary* questions are about the literary, or fiction, selection. The *expository* questions are about the expository, or nonfiction, selection. The *crossover* questions cover both the literary selection and the expository selection.

3. Before class, write several questions about a previously assigned reading on five to six pieces of chart paper, using the stems of the open-ended response questions from the Open-Ended Response Questions handout. Write one question at the top of each sheet of chart paper, and then post the charts around the room.

4. Place the students in groups of four to six. Explain that each chart has a different open-ended question that needs to be answered. Have each group stand next to a chart. Have one student from each group read the question on the group's chart.

5. Explain that each group will decide what are the best answers for its questions by discussing their ideas. The groups can write down as many answers as they can think of in the time given. The groups then rotate and add to each poster until all are filled out. Students cannot write something that another group has already written, and they must work as a team. One student in each group will be chosen to be the writer.

6. Time students so they have time to write a few good ideas, but not enough time to exhaust all the possibilities for other groups. Watch how much the groups write. After all groups have written on each chart, have each group choose its favorite home-chart answers by putting a star by each one. Each group then chooses a reporter to read their answers to the class.

7. For more practice, before class write several questions on a transparency about a previously assigned reading, using the stems of the open-ended response questions from the handout.

8. When beginning the classroom text discussion, have students open their ELA books to the selection to be discussed. Tell the students that there will be a new procedure for participating in class discussions. Display the text question on the overhead. Students should consider possible responses and then point to the text section that supports their answers. Call on a student for a response only after the teacher observes each student pointing to a text section. This procedure will increase the time after the question is posed, so every student will have the opportunity to formulate a response. It will also reinforce the process of providing textual evidence for their responses.

Plot Elements

Name: _____ Date: _____

Title of Story: _____

Exposition	**Setting:** What is the time and place of the story?	
	Characters: Who is the protagonist? Who is the antagonist?	
	Conflict: Internal Conflict External Conflict	
Rising Action	The series of events that happen to the character that create the conflicts	
Climax	The most intense moment in the story; the turning point, or the point when you know how the story will end	
Falling Action	The part of the story when the characters solve the problems caused by the conflict	
Resolution	The conclusion, or end of the story, in which the conflict is resolved	

Plot Elements Sort Cards

antagonist	The character who conflicts with the protagonist
conflict	A problem the story centers on; the struggle between opposing forces
climax	The turning point of the action or story
exposition	The background information about characters, conflict, and setting
external conflict	A problem outside the character
falling action/resolution	When the conflict ends and loose ends are tied up
internal conflict	A problem inside the character
plot	The sequence of events
protagonist	The hero or main character of the story
rising action	The complications that arise, making conflict more difficult to resolve
setting	The time and place of the story

Plot Elements Mountain

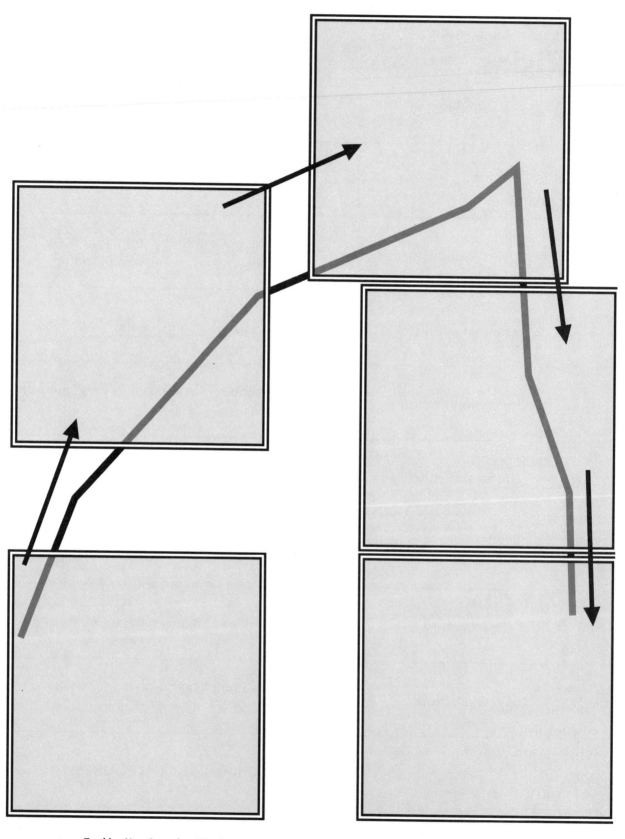

Plot Term Cards

Rising Action

The series of events that happen to the character that create the conflicts

Falling Action

The part of the story when the characters solve the problems caused by the conflict

Resolution

The conclusion, or end of the story, in which the conflict is resolved

Exposition

The beginning of the story. The introduction of the characters and setting

Climax

The most intense moment in the story; the turning point, or the point when you know how the story will end

Story Section Cards

Jack cuts down the beanstalk, and the giant falls and dies.	Jack steals the giant's goose, which lays golden eggs and runs away.
Jack lives with his poor mother in a small village. All they have is one cow.	Jack plants the beans and grows a gigantic beanstalk. He climbs the beanstalk and finds a giant's castle in the clouds.
Jack's mother sends him to town to trade the cow for food, and he trades the cow for some "magic" beans.	Jack and his mother are rich because they have the golden eggs.

Stick Figure Characterization

Thoughts
Explain what he or
she is thinking.

Speech
Tell what he
or she says.

Appearance
Describe how he or
she looks.

HELLO
My name is

Reactions of Others
Tell what others say or think.

Character Name
Write character's
name here.

Actions
Explain what he or she does.

Characterization Chart

Character Name — Write character's name here.	Appearance — Describe how he or she looks.	Actions — Explain what he or she does.	Thoughts — Explain what he or she is thinking.	Speech — Tell what he or she says.	Reactions of Others — Tell what others say or think.

Character Traits

1. active	27. cheerful	53. eager	79. grouchy
2. adventurous	28. childish	54. easygoing	80. grumpy
3. affectionate	29. clever	55. efficient	81. guilty
4. afraid	30. clumsy	56. embarrassed	82. happy
5. alert	31. concerned	57. encouraging	83. harsh
6. ambitious	32. confident	58. energetic	84. hateful
7. angry	33. confused	59. evil	85. healthy
8. annoyed	34. considerate	60. excited	86. helpful
9. anxious	35. cooperative	61. expert	87. honest
10. apologetic	36. courageous	62. fair	88. hopeful
11. arrogant	37. cowardly	63. faithful	89. hopeless
12. attentive	38. cruel	64. fearless	90. humorous
13. bad	39. curious	65. fierce	91. ignorant
14. bold	40. dangerous	66. foolish	92. imaginative
15. bored	41. daring	67. fortunate	93. impatient
16. bossy	42. decisive	68. friendly	94. impolite
17. brainy	43. demanding	69. frustrated	95. inconsiderate
18. brave	44. dependable	70. funny	96. independent
19. bright	45. depressed	71. gentle	97. industrious
20. brilliant	46. determined	72. giving	98. innocent
21. busy	47. discouraged	73. glamorous	99. intelligent
22. calm	48. dishonest	74. gloomy	100. jealous
23. careful	49. disrespectful	75. good	101. kind
24. careless	50. doubtful	76. graceful	102. lazy
25. cautious	51. dull	77. grateful	103. lively
26. charming	52. dutiful	78. greedy	104. lonely

continued

Character Traits (continued)

105. loving	124. poor	143. scared	162. talented
106. loyal	125. popular	144. secretive	163. tall
107. lucky	126. positive	145. selfish	164. thankful
108. mature	127. precise	146. serious	165. thoughtful
109. mean	128. proper	147. sharp	166. thoughtless
110. messy	129. proud	148. short	167. tired
111. miserable	130. quick	149. shy	168. tolerant
112. mysterious	131. quiet	150. silly	169. trusting
113. naughty	132. rational	151. skillful	170. trustworthy
114. nervous	133. reliable	152. sly	171. unfriendly
115. nice	134. religious	153. smart	172. unhappy
116. noisy	135. responsible	154. sneaky	173. upset
117. obedient	136. restless	155. sorry	174. useful
118. obnoxious	137. rich	156. spoiled	175. weak
119. old	138. rough	157. stingy	176. wicked
120. peaceful	139. rude	158. strange	177. wise
121. picky	140. sad	159. strict	178. worried
122. pleasant	141. safe	160. stubborn	179. wrong
123. polite	142. satisfied	161. sweet	180. young

Open-Ended Response Questions: Literary

Add the following statement to each question: "Support your answer with evidence from the selection."

What was one conflict _____ faced in "_____"?
(character)

In "_____," how does _____ connect to _____?

How does _____ change from the beginning to the end of "_____"?
(character)

What is the major conflict _____ faces in "_____"?
(character)

In "_____," what does _____ learn from his or her experience
(character)

with _____?

In "_____," why does _____
(character)

_____?
(action)

Who do you think has the greatest impact on _____: _____, _____,
(main character)   (list of minor characters)

or _____?

In "_____," what does the _____ symbolize to
(object)

_____?
(character)

continued

Open-Ended Response Questions: Literary (continued)

In "_____," what do _____ and _____ have in common?
(character)   (character)

How does _____ in "_____" show _____
(first character)   (feelings)
for _____?
(second character)

In "_____," do you think _____ gets what he or she
wants?   (character)

What does _____ symbolize in "_____"?

Explain how the narrator's actions reveal his or her feelings for _____ in
(character)
"_____."

Open-Ended Response Questions: Expository

Add the following statement to each question: "Support your answer with evidence from the selection."

In "_____," has _____ fulfilled his or her dream?
(character)

In "_____," how have the author's experiences shaped his or her attitude toward others?

How does the author's attitude toward _____ change over the course of (character) "_____"?

Why is "_____" a good title for this selection?

Why are memories of _____ important to _____?
(character) (character)

In "_____," who do you think is more successful, _____ (character) or _____?
(character)

Do you think _____ in "_____" is _____?
(character) (character trait) _____?

continued

Open-Ended Response Questions: Expository (continued)

How would you evaluate _____'s honesty in telling his or her story?
(character)

Why do you think _____ in "_____"?
(character)   (action)

Based on your reading of "_____," do you think _____
made the right decision?   (character)

In "_____," what does _____ learn from
_____?
(experience or other character)   (character)

Do you think _____ was a good _____?
(character)

How did _____ make _____ feel?
(experience)   (character)

In "_____," what is one way _____ is affected by
_____?
(experience)   (character)

Open-Ended Response Questions: Crossover

Add the following statement to each question: "Support your answer with evidence from both selections."

What impact does the point of view have in "_____" and

"_____"?

Do _____ in "_____" and _____ in
　　 (character)　　　　　　　　　　　　　　　　　　　　 (character)

"_____" share a similar concern?

How is _____ in "_____" similar to _____
　　　　 (character)　　　　　　　　　　　　　　　　　　　　　　　　　　 (character)

in "_____"?

What is one similarity between the actions of _____ in "_____"
　　　　　　　　　　　　　　　　　　　　　　　　 (character)

and the actions of _____ in "_____"?
　　　　　　　　　　　 (character)

Can _____ in "_____" and _____ in
　　 (character)　　　　　　　　　　　　　　　　　　　　　 (character)

"_____" be seen as intruders in these selections? Why or why not?

Are _____ in "_____" and _____ in
　　 (character)　　　　　　　　　　　　　　　　　　　　　 (character)

"_____" supported by their family members? Why or why not?

What do the narrators learn about their fathers/mothers/siblings/friends in

"_____" and "_____"?

continued

Open-Ended Response Questions: Crossover (continued)

How does the idea of taking a risk apply to both "_____" and

"_____"?

How do the parents in "_____" and "_____"

attempt to share their cultural heritage with their children?

Which of the siblings from "_____" and "_____

_____" would you like to have as a brother or sister? Why?

How is the concept/idea of _____ important in both "_____"

and "_____"?

What is one characteristic shared by _____ and
(character from literary passage)

_____?
(character from expository passage)

How is _____ an important theme in both "_____" and

"_____"?

Chapter 4

Teaching the ELA Academic Vocabulary

Six Principles of Vocabulary Development

There are several key principles that should guide the creation and implementation of an effective academic vocabulary development program.

1. Explicitly teach students the strategies for developing vocabulary.

Explicit instruction can be provided both formally through explicit vocabulary lessons and informally through various classroom interactions, such as reading aloud to students and having discussions and debates.

2. Connect new vocabulary terms to students' prior knowledge and experiences.

Students must be able to attach new words to words and concepts they already understand in order to contextualize their learning. If they are unable to do so, the new words will have little meaning to them. Without understanding meaning, students are only memorizing words for the weekly test.

3. Use new vocabulary words in the classroom.

Students should be able to use the newly learned vocabulary terms. For students to do this successfully, they must first be comfortable hearing and using these words in the classroom. Students should be encouraged or even required to incorporate new vocabulary terms into their oral presentations and written reports.

4. Practice and repeat new words.

Students should be exposed frequently to the same words through practice exercises, classroom use, and assessments. Practice and repetition are important methods to help students become familiar with new words and understand how they are used correctly.

5. Be enthusiastic and curious about new words yourself.

Look for "teachable moments" throughout the day when you can point out and collect words as they crop up in texts, stories, or conversations. Ask students to explore additional ways to express themselves using their new words. Through their own behaviors and attitudes, teachers can model an enthusiasm for learning new words.

6. Be committed to vocabulary development over the long term.

Teaching vocabulary must be interdisciplinary and incorporated into the curriculum at every level. Schools, teachers, and students must all make a commitment to vocabulary development.

Tips for Choosing Vocabulary List Words

Choose only five to ten words per week (per content area).

A secondary student has between six and eight different classes per semester, from computer applications and art to American history and geometry. Ten new words per class each week would total sixty to eighty new words per week, a healthy number not only to learn but also to try to retain. Furthermore, English language learners learn many more than ten words a week in their English as a Second Language class and acquire "survival" vocabulary (the social language used in school) every day in the halls, in the lunchroom, and on the bus. Even at only ten words per week, a student would be exposed to an annual total of 360 new vocabulary words per class, or 2,880 words for eight classes. This is an impressive 17,280 new words over the seven years of secondary school.

Choose "useful" words.

The vocabulary words listed at the beginning of each chapter in a textbook may not necessarily be the best ones to spend time teaching and learning. The student may never use them again after finishing that chapter. For example, the word *ibis* occurs in most vocabulary lists before the short story "The Scarlet Ibis," but it is hardly a word most students will use much. Also, students could figure out the word's meaning from the context of the story, which prominently features a large red bird. Far more useful would be the word *scarlet*, which does not appear on the textbook's vocabulary list and which students probably would not know. This is a word that students could use frequently, and it would be easy to reinforce throughout the year.

Choose words that the student will see again.

Many vocabulary words are used in multiple content areas, such as *scarlet* from the previous example. That word could appear in textbooks for English (*The Scarlet Letter*), science (scarlet macaw), social studies (scarlet fever), and possibly even in math word problems. Each time the student sees a word used in a different context it is reinforced, and retaining the word becomes more relevant. In the case of the word *scarlet*, its meaning—the color red—is the same across the content areas. However, some words have different meanings in different subjects, such as the word *table*. It is important to point out that words with more than one meaning may also occur as different parts of speech.

Using Word Walls

A *word wall* is an organized collection of words displayed on a classroom wall. The word wall is not for decoration; it is a tool to promote learning. There are many different ways to construct word walls, from putting words on index cards and placing them in a pocket chart to writing the words on a large piece of chart paper and taping it to the wall. Whatever its construction, the word wall serves as a permanent record of students' learning and provides ongoing support and a means for teaching the strategy of using a reference.

Lesson Plan for Using Word Walls

Materials

- WORDO Card handout, one per student (page 124)
- Vocabulary list of teacher-selected words
- Notebook paper
- Materials on which to write the vocabulary words, such as index cards, sentence strips, sticky notes, construction paper, or chart paper
- Comic strips, one per student
- Tape or glue
- Markers or colored pencils
- Transparency and overhead markers
- Two flashlights for Flashlight Relays (or two flyswatters for Flyswatter Relays)

Academic Vocabulary

Understanding the meaning of the following terms is critical to a student's success in this lesson. It will not be possible—or practical—to teach all the words on this list at once, nor is this an exhaustive list of vocabulary that is necessary to know for this lesson. Keep in mind that many students will already be familiar with many of these words.

bingo	feature	rhyme
caption	flashlight	search
clue	flyswatter	shine
comic	guess	sort
cover	organize	swat
crossword puzzle	pile	word wall
dictation	reference	

Activities

Refer to "Tips for Choosing Vocabulary List Words" on page 116 to learn how to select vocabulary to use in this lesson. The word-wall list can be created by the teacher and/or the students. The words can then be placed in alphabetical order or grouped according to different criteria, such as theme, unit, particular stories or books, or specialized words from the content areas. Place the word wall on a highly visible wall in the classroom to make it easily accessible for the activities, which can include (but are not limited to) those listed.

1. **Dictation**: Dictate sentences that contain words from the word wall. Allow the students to use the word wall as a reference. For a change of pace, ask students to take turns dictating sentences, using as many words from the word wall as possible.

2. **Read My Mind**: Have students get out a piece of paper and number the paper from one to five. Say, **I am thinking of a word.** Then give five clues about the word. The first clue is "The word is on the word wall." The second clue could be the number of letters in the word. After each clue, students try to guess the word-wall word and write it down next to the number of the clue given. When all clues have been given, ask students who "read your mind" first and guessed the correct word with the fewest clues. Do this activity with several words from the word wall, and then allow a student to choose a word, give the clues, and have his classmates "read his mind."

3. **Rhyme Time**: Give the students a word, and ask them to identify a rhyming word from the word wall. As an extension, have them write a poem using the rhyming words.

4. **Word Sorts**: Have students copy the words from the word wall on index cards or small slips of paper. Select word features, such as suffixes, vowel sounds, or beginning or ending letters. Challenge the students to sort and organize the words on their desks into different piles according to their word features. This is a good activity for small groups or pairs.

5. **Cartoon Captions**: Give students a collection of comics from the Sunday paper, and have them each choose a strip. Tell them to cut the strip apart and glue or tape three of the individual panels in sequence on a piece of paper. Then have the students write new captions under each of the panels or in the speech bubbles, using words from the word wall to create a story. Have students share their cartoon captions with the class.

6. **WORDO (Bingo)**: This game is played like Bingo. Give each student a copy of the WORDO Card handout. Have students fill in their cards with words from the word wall. Tell them to mix up the words they choose and make their card different from other students' cards. Call out a word, spell it or give its definition, and have the students mark their card if it contains that word. The first student to mark an entire row calls out "WORDO!" The winner gets to call out the words for the next round.

7. **Guess the Covered Word**: On a transparency on the overhead projector, write four or five sentences that contain a word from the word wall. Cover the word-wall words in the sentences with sticky notes or small slips of paper. Allow students to make several guesses for the word and then write their guesses on the board. Read the first sentence, substituting the students' guesses for the covered word, until the correct word is reached. Remove the sticky note covering that word and go to the next sentence, using the same procedure.

8. **Crossword Puzzles and Word Searches**: Use websites, such as www.wordplays.com or http://puzzlemaker.school.discovery.com to make crossword puzzles and word searches with words from the word wall.

9. **Categories**: Name a category, such as parts of speech, opposites, character descriptions, and so on, and ask students to call out words from the word wall that are in the given category. Alternately, ask the students to choose category topics according to the words that are on the word wall, and allow them to move the words until they are in their correct categories.

10. **Flashlight Relays (Flyswatter Relays)**: Have students form two teams and line up with each team facing the word wall. Give the first student in each team a flashlight. Turn off the lights in the room, and call out clues for a word on the word wall. The first student to shine the flashlight on the correct word wins a point for his or her team, and then the flashlight is passed to the next in line. Continue to call out clues and play the game until all the students have had a turn or all the words have been chosen. For a variation on this game, leave the lights on, and give students one flyswatter per team instead. Students will swat the correct word with the flyswatter.

The Importance of Vocabulary Notebooks

Vocabulary notebooks are not merely personal dictionaries. They are also books containing students' entries of words studied in teacher-directed lessons and encountered during independent reading.

The notebooks document the students' word study and vocabulary programs and help the teacher assess student activity and growth. Words in the notebooks can be grouped in various ways. Entering their vocabulary words in notebooks helps students organize their learning and teaches them a long-term strategy for using vocabulary in the classroom and beyond.

Lesson Plan for Vocabulary Notebooks

Materials

- Vocabulary Notebook handout, ten to twenty copies per student to start (page 125)

- Vocabulary list (eight to twelve words)

- Spiral notebooks, one per student

- Glue or tape

- Rulers

- Chart markers

- Chart paper

Academic Vocabulary

Understanding the meaning of the following terms is critical to a student's success in this lesson. It will not be possible—or practical—to teach all the words on this list at once, nor is this an exhaustive list of vocabulary that is necessary to know for this lesson. Keep in mind that many students will already be familiar with many of these words.

alphabetical order	dictionary	pronunciation
column	graphic	sentence
combination	illustration	spiral
connect	meaning	title
connection	notebook	vocabulary
definition		

Activities

At the beginning of the year, ask all students to purchase several bound notebooks (spiral or other) to be used for Vocabulary Notebooks throughout the year. Owning their own notebooks motivates students to both use and care for them. In lieu of spiral notebooks, teachers may distribute copies of the Vocabulary Notebook handout, hole-punched for students to place in a binder. Refer to "Tips for Choosing Vocabulary List Words" on page 116 to learn how to select vocabulary to use in this lesson.

1. Give a copy of the Vocabulary Notebook handout to each student. If necessary, tell students to trim the handout and glue or tape it to the inside front cover of their spiral notebook. On the first page of the notebook, have students create a title page with the title *Vocabulary Notebook,* their name, the teacher's name, and the class period.

2. Tell the students that the best way to learn new words is to use them in combination with words that they already know. Draw a large picture of the Vocabulary Notebook page on chart paper, and use it to demonstrate how to use the notebook to the class.

3. Explain to students that they are not simply making a dictionary of words in alphabetical order. They are creating a book to help them increase their vocabulary. The Vocabulary Notebook page (see table 4.1 on page 123 for an example) shows how they will divide each page of their vocabulary notebook. Have students draw the lines and label the columns as shown on the Vocabulary Notebook, starting on the front of the page following the title page. Tell the students to continue drawing the vocabulary notebook page on the front side only of the next ten pages.

4. In the first column on the chart paper, write the first vocabulary word to be learned. Pronounce the word for the students and have them repeat it. Have students copy the word into the first column in their notebooks. Next, have students write notes in the second column, in their first language about how to pronounce the word.

5. Dictionary definitions can be confusing to second language learners, so instead of using a dictionary to find meaning, explain the new word's meaning in simpler language and give several examples of its use. Then ask individual students to restate the word's explanation in their own words. Discuss the students' ideas, agree on a version of their definitions, and write it in the definition column on the chart paper. Instruct the students to create their own definition and write it in their notebook. It is important for the students to construct their own definition of the word using their own words rather than copying down the teacher's explanation.

6. After the word has been discussed and defined, explain that the next step is to create an illustration of the word, either by drawing a picture of it or using a graphic that helps the student understand the word. Ask the students what they would draw for this vocabulary word. Entertain many ideas, and invite a volunteer to draw his or her picture or graphic under the word on the chart paper.

7. Finally, point to the last column. Tell students that they will write their own sentences in this column using the word, and make connections to what they learn and hear. Discuss a possible sentence to use. After the class agrees on the sentence, write it down in the final column.

8. Ask the students what kinds of connections they can make to this word. Ask them questions, such as the following:

    • **Have you ever seen this word before?**

    • **Does it look like any other words you know?**

    • **Does it look like any words in your own language?**

    • **Can you think how we are going to use this word in class?**

    • **Can you think of other words that mean the same thing?**

    • **Can you think of other words that are connected in meaning to this word [such as *farm* and *country* with *pastoral*]?**

9. Record examples of student connections in the appropriate box on the chart paper. Have students write down as many connections as they want to help them remember the word. Tell students that additional connections they make later can be added as they watch and listen for each new word.

10. Have students form pairs to work together to complete their individual notebooks. Explain that they are to write and draw the things that will help them best remember the words. Tell them to look at their list of vocabulary words, beginning with the second word, and repeat the following process:

    • The teacher pronounces the word.

    • The students write down the word and its pronunciation in their own language.

    • The teacher describes the word and gives examples of its use in simple English.

    • The partners discuss the word's meaning, determine its definition in their own words, and write down the definition.

    • The partners discuss an illustration or graphic for the word, and then each draws their own.

    • The partners discuss possible sentences using the word and then they each write a sentence in their own words.

11. When all words have been completed, have students select a new partner. Ask students to share with their new partner what they wrote and drew. Allow students to add to or change their information as they work together with new partners.

12. During the week, provide opportunities for the students to review and add to their knowledge about the words, make connections to and interact with each other about them, and play games with them.

Table 4.1: Example of a Filled-Out Vocabulary Notebook Page

New Word and Illustration	Pronunciation	Definition in Your Own Words.	Sentence and/or Connections
pastoral	pastoral	life in the beautiful country, peaceful, simple	pastor at church, pastor in Spanish means shepherd
scarlet	scarlet	the color red, it can represent sin	The "Scarlet Ibis" short story, The Scarlet Letter novel, a school color
threat	thret	a danger, warning that something bad will happen	On the news they said there was a threat of thunderstorms.
replicate	replikate	to make an exact copy of something	In Science class, we replicated a famous experiment—we copied it.

WORDO Card

W	O	R	D	O

W	O	R	D	O

Vocabulary Notebook

New Word and Illustration	Pronunciation	Definition in Your Own Words	Sentence and/or Connections

Appendix

The ELA Academic Vocabulary Word Lists

Literary Terms

allusion

analogy

antagonist

author

autobiography

biography

character

comedy

comic relief

conflict

context

dialect

dialogue

drama

element

exposition

falling action

figurative language

flashback

foreshadow

imagery

irony

meaning

melody

metaphor

mood

narrative

narrator

paradox

personification

plot

poetry

point of view

protagonist

relevance

resolution

rising action

rhythm

setting

short story

simile

structure

suspense

symbol

theme

time frame

tone

tragedy

Revising and Editing Terms

add

any

change

combine

correction

could

delete

document

draft

editing

effective

fill in

follow

idea

improve

improvement

insert

logically

made

move

organization

paper

paragraph

passage

review

revise

revising

revision

rewrite

rough draft

sentence

should

support

switch

transition

Reading Terms

advertisement

analogy

antonym

background

bias

cause and effect

characteristic

chart

chronological order

cite

classic

colonial

compare and contrast

comprehend

conclusion

connotation

contemporary

context

craft

credibility

critique

culture

database

deceptive

deconstruct

deduction

denotation

derivation

dialogue

diary

dictionary

discussion

documentary

drama

edit

editorial

faulty

figurative language

film

generalization

genre

glittering generalities

glossary

graph

graphic organizer

heading

historical context

homonym

idealism

idiom

index

induction

inference

influence

interpret

journal

literary

literature

logical

logical fallacies

main idea

map

meaning

media

memoranda

mode

motivation

multiple-meaning word

narrator

naturalism

newspaper

novel

organization

outline (verb)

overview

period

periodical

persuasion

poetry

precolonial

prediction

prefix

realism

relevant

reread

resource

response

review

revolutionary

romanticism

root

scan

skim

speech

story

strategy

study guide

suffix

summarize

supporting details

synonym

syntax

text

thesaurus

vocabulary

word origin

Purpose for Reading

to appreciate a writer's craft

to be entertained

to be informed

to discover

to discover models to use

to enjoy

to find out

to interpret

to solve problems

to take action

to understand reference

Writing Terms

abstract (noun)

audience

Author's Purpose

to compare

to describe

to entertain

to explain

to express

to influence

to inform

to persuade

body

capitalization

clarity

coherent

compose

composition

conclusion

content

conventions

create

depth

draft

edit

ellipses

essay

expression

evidence

general

grammar

introduction

italics

literary

logical argument

logical progression

manual of style

mechanics

memo

narrative

occasion

opinion

organization

parallelism

persuasive

play

poem

prewriting

procedure

process

proofread

publish

punctuation

purpose

reflective

report

response

résumé

revise

sentence

source

specific

spelling

story

structure

style

summary

supporting idea

thesis

topic

voice

word choice

Viewing and Representing Terms

ad campaign

advertisement

analysis

attitude

audience

camera angles

communicate

compare

construct

content

contrast

convey

coverage

critique

culture

deconstruct

design

distinguish

documentary

editing

editorial

effect

element

engage

entertaining text

examine

evaluate

event

feedback form

flyer

generalization

genre

group discussion

idea

informative text

Internet

interpret

investigate

line

main idea

media

message

music

news magazine

newspaper

nightly news

perception

photograph

political campaign

presentation

print ad

product

production

property

purpose

questionnaire

reaction shots

reality

reflect

relationship

represent

response

sequencing

shape

significance

source

special effects

specific

technique

technology

television

texture

unique

video

video adaptation

view

visual representation

web page

Test Question Vocabulary

actions

affect

agree

answer

appear

attitude

avoid

besides

best

choose

compare

concept

conclude

convey

convince

definition

describe

description

develop

disclose

drawing

effective

entry

experience (noun)

experience (verb)

explain

express	notes	summary
evidence	over the course	support
figure out	paragraph	tell
follow	persuade	throughout
following	primary	understand
generalization	prove	use
highlight	purpose	view
illustrate	reader	
illustration	respond	
impact	response	
imply	reveal	
indicate	selection	
mainly	sentiment	
major	show	
match	significance	
mean	similar	
meaning	structure	
mostly	suggest	
narrator	summarize	

References and Resources

Allen, J. (1999). *Words, words, words*. York, ME: Stenhouse Publishers.

Allen, J. (2002, September). Test-smart language users: Understanding the language of testing. *Voices from the Middle, 10*(1), 56–57.

Beck, I. L. (2002). *Bringing words to life*. New York: The Guilford Press.

Bielenberg, B., & Fillmore, L. W. (2004, December/2005, January). The English they need. *Educational Leadership, 62*(4), 45–49.

Blachowicz, C., & Fisher, P. J. (2002). *Teaching vocabulary in all classrooms*. Upper Saddle River, NJ: Pearson Education.

Burke, J. (2004, May). Learning the language of academic study. *Voices from the Middle, 11*(4), 37–42.

Chamot, A. U., & O'Malley, J. M. (1994). *The CALLA handbook*. New York: Addison-Wesley.

Coxhead, A. (2000). A new academic word list. *Teachers of English to Speakers of Other Languages Quarterly, 34*(2), 213–238.

Coxhead, A., & Nation, P. (2001). The specialised vocabulary of English for academic purposes. In J. Flowerdew & M. Peacock (Eds.), *Research perspectives on English for academic purposes* (pp. 252–267). Cambridge, England: Cambridge University Press.

Cruz, M. (2004, March). Can English language learners acquire academic English? *English Journal, 93*(4), 14–17.

Cruz, M. (2005, July). Do our students really speak the language of the test? *English Journal, 94*(6), 15–17.

Cummins, J. (1983). Language proficiency and academic achievement. In J. W. Oller, Jr. (Ed.), *Issues in language testing research* (pp. 108–129). Rowley, MA: Newbury House.

Cunningham, P. (2004). *Phonics they use: Words for reading and writing* (4th ed.). Boston: Allyn & Bacon.

Echevarria, J., Short, D. J., & Vogt, M. (2004). *Making content comprehensible for English language learners: The SIOP model* (2nd ed.). Boston: Allyn & Bacon.

Ediger, M. (1999). Reading and vocabulary development. *Journal of Instructional Psychology, 26*(1), 7–15.

Hamel, B. H. (2004). *Comprehensive bilingual dictionary of false cognates* (2nd ed.). Beverly Hills, CA: Bilingual Book Press.

Harvey, S., & Goudvis, A. (2000). *Strategies that work: Teaching comprehension to enhance understanding.* York, ME: Stenhouse Publishers.

Laflamme, J. G. (1997). The effect of multiple exposure vocabulary method and the target reading/writing strategy on test scores. *Journal of Adolescent & Adult Literacy, 40*(5), 372–384.

Marzano, R. J. (2004). *Building background knowledge for academic achievement.* Alexandria, VA: Association for Supervision and Curriculum Development.

Marzano, R. J. (2005). *Building academic vocabulary.* Alexandria, VA: Association for Supervision and Curriculum Development.

McClure, C. T. (2007, May). Reading and verbal skills are not enough. *Teachers Teaching Teachers, 2*(8), 9–10.

Ragan, A. (2005, November/December). Teaching the academic language of textbooks: A preliminary framework for performing a textual analysis. *The ELL Outlook, 4*(5). Accessed at http://coursecrafters.com/ELL-Outlook/2005/nov_dec/ on April 20, 2007.

Real Academia Española. (2005). *Diccionario panhispánico de dudas.* Bogotá, Colombia: Santillana.

r4 Educated Solutions. (2006a). *TAKS open-ended responses guide grades 9–11 exit* (2nd ed.). Houston, TX: Author.

r4 Educated Solutions. (2009). *Teaching your secondary English language learners the academic language of tests: Focusing on language in mathematics, science, and social studies.* Bloomington, IN: Solution Tree Press.

r4 Educated Solutions. (2006c). *Vocabulary instruction for intermediate English language learners: Teaching students in English, ESOL, and ESL classrooms.* Houston, TX: Author.

Spangenberg-Urbschat, K., & Pritchard, R. (Eds.). (1994). *Kids come in all languages: Reading instruction for ESL students.* Newark, DE: International Reading Association.

Texas Reading Initiative. (2000). *Promoting vocabulary development: Components of effective vocabulary instruction.* Austin, TX: Texas Education Agency.

Whitehurst, G. J. (2002). *Evidence-based education (EBE)*. Presentation at the Student Achievement and School Accountability Conference. Accessed at ed.gov/nclb/methods/whatworks/eb/edlite-slide003.html on January 4, 2006.

Woods, R. D., & Stovall, M. M. (2005). *Spanish-English cognates*. New York: University Press of America.

Index

Solution Tree | Press

a division of

Solution Tree

Solution Tree's mission is to advance the work of our authors. By working with the best researchers and educators worldwide, we strive to be the premier provider of innovative publishing, in-demand events, and inspired professional development designed to transform education to ensure that all students learn.

The core purpose of Region 4 is revolutionizing education to inspire and advance future generations™. Instructional materials such as this publication are written and reviewed by content-area specialists who have an array of experience in providing quality, effective classroom instruction that provides the most impact on student achievement.

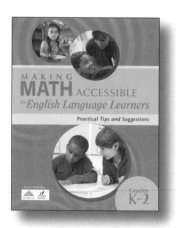 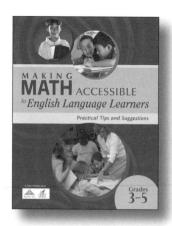 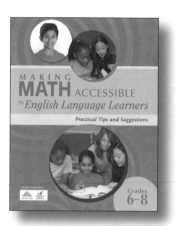 

Making Math Accessible for English Language Learners Series
By r4 Educated Solutions
Build the academic language English language learners need to gain proficiency in mathematics. These practical classroom tips and suggestions provide a solid plan for bringing disadvantaged learners up to speed with essential vocabulary while keeping the entire class engaged with the lessons.

Grades K–2
BKF284

Grades 3–5
BKF285

Grades 6–8
BKF286

Grades 9–12
BKF287

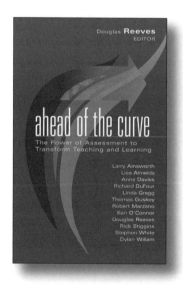

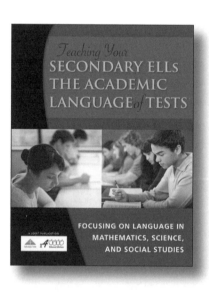

Ahead of the Curve: The Power of Assessment to Transform Teaching and Learning
Edited by Douglas Reeves
Get the anthology that offers the ideas and recommendations of many of the world's leaders in assessment. Many perspectives of effective assessment design and implementation culminate in a call for redirecting assessment to improve student achievement and inform instruction.
BKF232

Teaching Your Secondary English Language Learners the Academic Language of Tests: Focusing on English Language Arts
By r4 Educated Solutions
Teach your English language learners unfamiliar language features before they are encountered in core content areas and standardized test questions. Evidence-based, teacher-friendly lesson plans also support content-area teachers in providing instruction for content-specific language skills.
BKF292